Moral Relativism and Moral Objectivity

Great Debates in Philosophy
Series Editor: Ernest Sosa

Dialogue has always been a powerful means of philosophical exploration and exposition. By presenting important current issues in philosophy in the form of a debate, this series attempts to capture the flavour of philosophical argument and to convey the excitement generated by the exchange of ideas. Each author contributes a major, original essay. When these essays have been completed, the authors are each given the opportunity to respond to the opposing view.

Moral Relativism and Moral Objectivity

Gilbert Harman
Judith Jarvis Thomson

BLACKWELL *Publishers*

First published 1996

Reprinted 1996, 1997

Blackwell Publishers Inc
Commerce Place, 350 Main Street,
Malden, Massachusetts 02148, USA

Blackwell Publishers Ltd
108 Cowley Road
Oxford OX4 1JF, UK

Library of Congress Cataloging in Publication Data
Harman, Gilbert
Moral relativism and moral objectivity/Gilbert Harman, Judith Jarvis Thomson
p. cm. — (Great debates in philosophy)
Includes bibliographical references and index.
ISBN 0–631–19209–3 (hbk:alk. paper) — ISBN 0–631–19211–5 (pbk:alk. paper)
1. Ethics. 2. Ethical relativism. 3. Objectivity. I. Thomson, Judith Jarvis.
II. Title. III. Series.
BJ1012.H316   1996   95–12472
171'7—dc20   CIP

British Library Cataloguing in Publication Data
A CIP catalogue record for this book is available from the British Library

Typeset in 10.5 on 13pt Melior
by Pure Tech India Ltd., Pondicherry, India
Printed and bound in Great Britain by Hartnolls Ltd, Bodmin, Cornwall

This book is printed on acid-free paper

Dedicated to
Marguerite and William Harman
Theodore and Mildred Jarvis

Contents

Preface

The history of philosophy is a history of debate. Like scientists, philosophers try to make sense of the world, but the sense they try to make of it is different. Scientists try to find out what the world is in fact like, and why. Scientists begin with things visible to the naked eye, and then go below and beyond them: they ask what that is too small or too distant to be seen by the naked eye explains them. They use microscopes and telescopes in doing so, and their hypotheses are confirmed or disconfirmed by the use of better, more sophisticated microscopes and telescopes. Philosophers also begin with things visible to the naked eye, but what they ask is not what explains them, but rather what would constitute explaining them. Their only equipment is pure reason, and their hypotheses are confirmed or disconfirmed only by the exercise of better reasoning. Scientists do not debate whether a scientific theory is sound, they look and see. Philosophers do, indeed must, expose their philosophical theories to rebuttal, since it is only in that way that they can find out whether there was a mistake in the reasoning that made their theories seem plausible.

What follows is a debate in moral philosophy. Moral philosophy is a large territory; the area of it in which our debate takes place is sometimes called meta-ethics. Anthropologists, sociologists, psychologists, and biologists try to find out what moral views are held by which groups of people, and why they are held. The moral philosopher who works in meta-ethics is trying to find out what would constitute explaining the fact that people hold moral views. Is our having moral views the product of our having observed moral facts? (Are there any moral facts?) Or is our having them merely a matter of our having certain attitudes toward nonmoral facts?

In short, we will not be debating the question which set of moral views is correct; alternatively put, we will not be debating the question which ethic is correct. Rather we will be debating the question whether there is any such thing as an ethic's being correct – hence the name meta-ethics for the enterprise we are engaged in. Harman takes the view that there is no such thing as an ethic's being correct; Thomson says that there is.

Parts I and II were written independently of each other, Part I (chapters 1–5) by Harman, Part II (chapters 6–8) by Thomson. Part III contains our responses to each other: in chapter 9, Harman responds to Thomson's Part II; in chapter 10, Thomson responds to Harman's Part I. As is the wont of the practicing philosopher, Harman and Thomson would have liked to go on with the debate. We envisaged a series of further chapters, containing responses to the responses to the responses . . . and so on. Fortunately, no doubt, the constraint imposed by the structure of volumes in the series made that impossible. We think in any case that it is best for students – for whom we are writing throughout – that they form their own views about the merits of ours.

Both of us are grateful for comments and criticism by others. Harman is indebted to comments on earlier drafts by Judith Jarvis Thomson, Samuel Wheeler, Margaret Gilbert, Nicholas Sturgeon, Garrett Deckel, Stuart Brock, Christian Pillar, and Elizabeth Harman. Preparation of the initial version of his part of the manuscript was supported in part by a grant to Princeton University from the James S. McDonnell Foundation.

Thomson thanks the members of her seminar in Moral Philosophy at MIT (Fall 1994) for comments on what she had (mistakenly) thought would be its final draft: Alexander Byrne, Kouji Hashimoto, Miguel Hernando, Timothy Hinton, Erica Klempner, Josep Macia, Dean Pettit, Michael Ridge, John Tully, Gabriel Uzquiano. Parts of earlier versions were helpfully criticized by many people; she is particularly grateful to Joshua Cohen, Catherine Elgin, Gilbert Harman, Kathrin Koslicki, and Daniel Stoljar. An early version of parts of chapters 8 and 10 was presented as the Immanuel Kant Lectures at Stanford University in May 1994; Thomson is grateful to those who participated for their comments and criticism.

GH and JJT

Part I
Moral Relativism

Gilbert Harman

1

Moral Relativism

1.1 Introduction

Motion is a relative matter. Motion is always relative to a choice of spatio-temporal framework. Something that is moving in relation to one spatio-temporal framework can be at rest in relation to another. And no spatio-temporal framework can be singled out as the one and only framework that captures the truth about whether something is in motion.

According to Einstein's Theory of Relativity even an object's mass is relative to a choice of spatio-temporal framework. An object can have one mass in relation to one such framework and a different mass in relation to another. Again, there is no privileged spatio-temporal framework that determines the real mass of an object.

I am going to argue for a similar claim about moral right and wrong. That is, in my contribution to this book I am going to defend *moral relativism*. I am going to argue that moral right and wrong (good and bad, justice and injustice, virtue and vice, etc.) are always relative to a choice of moral framework. What is morally right in relation to one moral framework can be morally wrong in relation to a different moral framework. And no moral framework is objectively privileged as the one true morality.

Einstein's relativistic conception of mass involves the following claim about the truth conditions of judgments of mass.

(1) For the purposes of assigning truth conditions, a judgment of the form, *the mass of X is M* has to be understood as elliptical for a judgment of the form, *in relation to spatio-temporal framework F the mass of X is M.*

The word *elliptical* might be misleading here. Einstein's Theory of Relativity does not involve a claim about meaning or about what people intend to be claiming when they make judgments about an object's mass. The point is, rather, that the only truth there is in this area is relative truth.

Before Einstein, judgments about mass were not intended as relative judgments. But it would be mean-spirited to invoke an "error theory" and conclude that these pre-Einsteinian judgments were all false![1] Better to suppose that such a judgment was true to the extent that an object had the relevant mass in relation to a spatio-temporal framework that was conspicuous to the person making the judgment, for example, a framework in which that person was at rest.

Similarly, the moral relativism I will argue for is not a claim what people *mean* by their moral judgments. Moral relativism does not claim that people intend their moral judgments to be "elliptical" in the suggested way; just as relativism about mass does not claim that people intend their judgments about mass to make implicit reference to a spatio-temporal framework.

To a first approximation, moral relativism makes the following claim about moral judgments.

(2) For the purposes of assigning truth conditions, a judgment of the form, *it would be morally wrong of P to D,* has to be understood as elliptical for a judgment of the form, *in relation to moral framework M, it would be morally wrong of P to D.* Similarly for other moral judgments.[2]

---

[1] Mackie, 1977, chapter one, advocates an error theory of this sort about ordinary moral judgments.

[2] So, for example, a judgment of the form, *P ought morally to D*, has to be understood as elliptical for a judgment of the form, *in relation to moral framework M, P ought morally to D.*

As before, it is important not to put too much stress on the word *elliptical*. The moral relativism I will argue for is no more a claim about what people mean by their moral judgments than relativism about mass is a claim about what people mean when they make judgments about mass. Moral relativism does not claim that people intend their moral judgments to be "elliptical" in the suggested way; just as relativism about mass does not claim that people intend their judgments about mass to make implicit reference to a spatio-temporal framework.

I use (2) as a first approximation to part of a definition of moral relativism. In chapter 3 below I discuss a complication that arises from the possibility that moral relativism may be compatible with a certain sort of "quasi-absolutism" that complicates the picture by allowing for nonobjective truth conditions.

1.1.1 Relativism, Absolutism, and Nihilism

(2) is only part of a definition of moral relativism because it is important to distinguish moral relativism both from moral absolutism on the one side and from moral nihilism on the other side. Moral absolutism holds that there is a single true morality. Moral relativism claims instead:

(3) There is no single true morality. There are many different moral frameworks, none of which is more correct than the others.

Moral nihilism agrees with (3) and takes that conclusion to be a reason to reject morality altogether including any sort of relative morality.

Moral nihilism can be compared to religious nihilism. Religious nihilism would be a natural response to the conclusion that there is no single true religion but only many different religious outlooks, none of which is more correct than the others. Such a conclusion would seem to provide a reason to reject religion and religious judgments altogether, rather than a reason to accept "religious relativism." It might then be

possible to assign objective truth conditions to religious judgments in relation to one or another religious framework, but it
is hard to see how such relative religious judgments could play
a serious role in religious practices. Moral nihilism argues that
the same is true of morality: given (3), there is no point to
engaging in morality and moral judgment.

Moral relativism rejects moral nihilism and asserts instead

(4) Morality should not be abandoned.

Furthermore, moral relativism insists (in opposition to emotivism and quasi-absolutism, discussed in chapter 3, below).

(5) Relative moral judgments can continue to play a serious
role in moral thinking.

1.1.2 Plan

In the next two sections of this chapter, 1.2 and 1.3, I mainly
argue against moral absolutism and in favor of (3). In particular,
I argue that (3) is made very plausible by actual moral diversity.
In sections 1.4 and 1.5 I discuss the sort of relativity involved
in moral relativism.

In chapter 2, I will begin to respond to moral nihilism by
arguing that morality is needed for reasons similar to the reasons for which law is needed. This leads me to elaborate a
version of moral conventionalism according to which even the
most basic aspects of morality are conventional in something
like the way in which I suppose law is conventional.

Some theorists hold that law is not completely conventional,
and that law is an attempt to formalize certain aspects of a
nonconventional morality, a view sometimes associated with
the notion of "Natural Law." Since I believe that morality is
completely conventional, it should be evident that I also reject
a nonconventional account of law.

Of course, there are obvious differences between law and
morality. Law requires a relatively formal legal system that is
recognized by a determinate group of people. Moral conven-

tions are less determinate than legal conventions and it is less clear who belongs to the relevant group. There are shifting groups with changing moral conventions. Different conventions are appropriate in one's family, in the local neighborhood, with co-workers, with friends, and with strangers in one's society. There is even a limiting case (in morality, not in law) where a person sets standards for him or herself – a one-person group.

As I envision law, the content of law is not fixed in advance of all human decision. People decide what the law will be, often as a result of some sort of bargaining. Bargaining allows people to reach agreement on something on which there is no antecedently right answer. For example, when two people bargain over the price of a rug at a garage sale, they do not engage in an inquiry into the right price for the rug. They may appeal to various facts about the rug, about the financial condition of the bargainers, about their other options, and about their desires concerning the rug. But the price of the rug is not determined in advance of their bargaining. Nor is the content of law determined in advance of the bargaining among those who make the law. I believe that the same is true of morality. Morality is itself the result of a kind of bargaining, or so I will argue in chapter 2.

Chapter 3 takes up complications arising from the suggestion already mentioned that there is an emotivist or quasi-absolutist way of using moral language that is (a) compatible with moral relativism, but (b) allows relativists with different moralities to express disagreements in moral attitude directly. As we shall see, the possibility of using moral language in the suggested way makes it more difficult to offer an adequate statement of moral relativism. It also challenges the moral relativist's claim in (5) that relative moral judgments are useful.

In chapter 4 I consider what relativists should say about moral reasons people have to act in various ways, and in chapter 5 I discuss what implications moral relativism might have for tolerance of those with different moral outlooks. Both of these issues are made more difficult by the considerations discussed in chapter 3.

1.2 Explaining Moral Diversity

In this and the following section I argue that the following claim is a reasonable inference from the most plausible explanation of moral diversity.

> There is no single true morality. There are many different moral frameworks, none of which is more correct than the others.

I begin by mentioning data to be explained: the nature and extent of moral diversity.

Members of different cultures often have very different beliefs about right and wrong and often act quite differently on their beliefs. To take a seemingly trivial example, different cultures have different rules of politeness and etiquette: burping after eating is polite in one culture, impolite in another. Less trivially, some people are cannibals, others find cannibalism abhorrent.

The institution of marriage takes different forms in different societies. In some, a man is permitted to have several wives, in others bigamy is forbidden. More generally, the moral status of women varies greatly from one society to another in many different ways.

Some societies allow slavery, some have caste systems, which they take to be morally satisfactory, others reject both slavery and caste systems as grossly unjust.

It is unlikely that any nontrivial moral principles are universally accepted in all societies. The anthropologist George Silberbauer (1993, p. 15) is able to say only that "there are values which can be seen as common to nearly all societies," a remark limited by the phrases "can be seen as" and "nearly all." He further limits this claim by adding, "there are sometimes strong contrasts in the ways in which [these values] are expressed in precepts, principles and evaluations of behaviour."

Some say that there is a universally recognized central core of morality consisting of prohibitions against killing and harming others, against stealing, and against lying to others. Walzer (1987, p. 24) offers a more limited list of universal prohibitions:

"murder, deception, betrayal and gross cruelty." It makes sense for Walzer to leave theft off the list, since some societies do not recognize private property, so they would have no rules against stealing. (Without property, there can be no such thing as stealing. It is trivial to say that all societies that recognize private property have rules against stealing, because having such rules is a necessary condition of recognizing private property!)

It may be that *murder* is always considered wrong, if murder is defined as "wrongful killing." But few societies accept *general* moral prohibitions on killing or harming other people. There are societies in which a "master" is thought to have an absolute right to treat his slaves in any way he chooses, including arbitrarily beating and killing them. Similarly, there may be no limitations on what a husband can do to his wife, or a father to his young children. Infanticide is considered acceptable in some societies. When moral prohibitions on harming and killing and lying exist, they are sometimes supposed to apply only with respect to the local group and not with respect to outsiders. A person who is able successfully to cheat outsiders may be treated as an admirable person. Similarly for someone who is able to harm and kill outsiders.

Any universally accepted principle in this area must verge on triviality, saying, for example, that one must not kill or harm members of a certain group, namely the group of people one must not kill or harm![3]

Thomson (1990) appears to disagree. She states certain principles and says of them, "it is not at all clear how their negations could be accommodated into what would be recognizable as a moral code" (Thomson, 1990, p. 20). The principles she mentions are, "Other things being equal, one ought not act rudely,"

---

[3] There will be universal truths about moralities just as there are universal truths about spatio-temporal frameworks. Perhaps all spatio-temporal frameworks must admit of motion and rest. And perhaps all moralities have some rules against killing, harm, and deception. The existence of universal features of spatio-temporal frameworks is compatible with and is even required by Einstein's Theory of Relativity and the existence of universal features of morality is compatible with moral relativism.

"Other things being equal, one ought to do what one promised," "Other things being equal, one ought not cause others pain," and "One ought not torture babies to death for fun."

On the contrary, it is clear that many moral codes have accommodated the negations of all these general principles by accepting instead principles restricted to insiders. And, if the phrase "other things being equal" is supposed to include a restriction to insiders, then triviality looms in the manner I have already mentioned.

Now, mere moral diversity is not a disproof of moral absolutism. Where there are differences in custom, there are often differences in circumstance. Indeed, differences in custom are themselves differences in circumstance that can affect what is right or wrong without entailing moral relativism. You do not need to be a moral relativist to recognize that in England it is wrong to drive on the right, whereas in France it is not wrong to drive on the right.

Even where circumstances are relevantly the same, mere differences in moral opinion no more refute moral absolutism than scientific differences in opinion about the cause of canal-like features on the surface of Mars establish that there is no truth to that matter.

But, even though the rejection of moral absolutism is not an immediate logical consequence of the existence of moral diversity, it is a reasonable inference from the most *plausible explanation* of the range of moral diversity that actually exists (Wong, 1984).

One of the most important things to explain about moral diversity is that it occurs not just between societies but also within societies and in a way that leads to seemingly intractable moral disagreements. In the contemporary United States, deep moral differences often seem to rest on differences in basic values rather than on differences in circumstance or information. Moral vegetarians, who believe that it is wrong to raise animals for food, exist in the same community as nonvegetarians, even in the same family. A disagreement between moral vegetarians and nonvegetarians can survive full discussion and full information and certainly appears to rest on a difference in the significance assigned to animals as compared with humans.

Is there a nonrelative truth concerning the moral importance of animals? How might that "truth" be discovered?

In a similar way, disagreements about the moral acceptability of abortion or euthanasia survive extensive discussion and awareness of all relevant information about abortion. Such disagreements appear to depend on basic disagreements concerning the intrinsic value or "sanctity" of human life as compared with the value of the things that life makes possible, such as pleasurable experience and fulfilling activity (Dworkin, 1993).

There are similarly intractable disagreements about the relative value of artifacts of culture as compared with human life. Some people think that it is worse when terrorists bomb famous old museums than when they bomb crowded city streets; others feel that the loss of human life is worse than the loss of architecture and art. Again, there are disagreements about how much help one person should be prepared to give to others. Is it morally wrong to purchase a new record player instead of trying to help people who cannot afford food? Singer (1972) says yes; others say no. There are intractable disputes about whether it is morally worse to kill someone than it is to let that person die (Rachels, 1975) and about the relative importance of liberty versus equality in assessing the justice of social arrangements (Rawls, 1971; Nozick, 1972).

Furthermore, some people in the United States and elsewhere are strict egoists in the sense that they are concerned only with what is to be gained for themselves. These are not just people who give in to temptation, but rather people who think it is stupid and irrational not to restrict their activities to "looking out for number one" (Ringer, 1977). They see no point in telling the truth to others, to helping others in time of need, in keeping agreements with others, or in avoiding injury or even death to others, apart from expected gain to themselves. Many other people disagree with egoism, believing that there are often reasons to keep agreements, etc., even when doing so is not in one's interest.

It is hard to see how to account for all moral disagreements in terms of differences in situation or beliefs about nonmoral facts. Many moral disagreements seem to rest instead on basic differences in moral outlook.

1.3 Explaining Basic Differences

Suppose that many moral disagreements do indeed rest on basic differences in moral outlook rather than on differences in situation or beliefs about nonmoral facts. What explanation might there be for that?

An "absolutist" explanation might be that some people are simply not well placed to discover the right answers to moral questions.[4] The point to this response is not just that different people have different evidence but that what one makes of evidence depends on one's antecedent beliefs, so that starting out with some beliefs can help one reach the truth, whereas starting out with other beliefs can prevent one from reaching the truth. Rational change in belief tends to be conservative. It is rational to make the least change in one's view that is necessary in order to obtain greater coherence in what one believes (Goodman, 1965; Rawls, 1971; Harman, 1986). Different people with different starting points will rationally respond in different ways to the same evidence. There is no guarantee that people who start sufficiently far apart in belief will tend to converge in view as the evidence comes in. Someone whose initial view is relatively close to the truth may be led by the evidence to come closer to the truth. Someone who starts further away from the truth may be led even further away by the same evidence. Such a person is simply not well placed to discover the truth.

Here then is an one absolutist's explanation of why moral disagreements that rest on basic differences in moral outlook cannot be rationally resolved, supposing that is in fact the case.

Moral relativists instead see an analogy with other kinds of relativity.

Consider the ancient question whether the earth moves or the sun moves. Here the relativistic answer is correct. Motion is a relative matter. Something can be in motion relative to one system of spatio-temporal coordinates and not in motion

---

[4] I am indebted to Nicholas Sturgeon for this suggestion.

relative to another system. The particular motion an object exhibits will differ from one system to another. There is no such thing as absolute motion, apart from one or another system of coordinates.

A relativistic answer is also plausible in the moral case. Moral right and wrong are relative matters. A given act can be right with respect to one system of moral coordinates and wrong with respect to another system of moral coordinates. And nothing is absolutely right or wrong, apart from any system of moral coordinates.

By "a moral system of coordinates" I mean a set of values (standards, principles, etc.), perhaps on the model of the laws of one or another state. Whether something is wrong in relation to a given system of coordinates is to determined by the system together with the facts of the case in something like the way in which whether something is illegal in a given jurisdiction is determined by the laws of that jurisdiction together with the facts of the case.

Why does it seem (to some people) that there are objective nonrelative facts about moral right and wrong? Well, why does it seem to some people that there objective nonrelative facts about motion or mass? In the case of motion or mass, one particular system of coordinates is so salient that it seems to have a special status. Facts about motion or mass in relation to the salient system of coordinates are treated as nonrelational facts.

In a similar way, the system of moral coordinates that is determined by a person's own values can be so salient that it can seem to that person to have a special status. Facts about what is right or wrong in relation to that system of coordinates can be misdentified as objective nonrelational facts.

To be sure, the system of moral coordinates that is determined by a given person's values cannot in general be *identified* with all and only exactly those very values. Otherwise a person could never be mistaken about moral issues (in relation to the relevant system of coordinates) except by being mistaken about his or her own values!

For the same reason, a legal system cannot be simply identified with existing legislation, the record of prior court decisions, and the principles currently accepted by judges.

Otherwise legislation could not be unconstitutional and judges could not be mistaken in the legal principles they accept or the decisions they reach.

It is a complex and unresolved, issue just how actual current law is related to or determined by existing legislation, prior court decisions, and accepted legal principles (Dworkin, 1986, offers one answer.). Similarly, there is no single agreed on answer on how a given person's values determine a moral system, a system of moral coordinates. Different moral relativists may have different theories about this, just as different legal theorists have different theories about the corresponding issue about law.

A moral relativist might wish to identify the moral system determined by a given person's values with a system of "corrected values." These corrected values would be the values that would result if the person were rationally to revise his or her values in the light of the facts, adjusting the values in order to make them more coherent with each other and with the facts. To be sure, this identification is vague and different moral relativists who accept this identification will interpret it differently.

Any relativist who accepts such an identification will claim, of course, that when different people correct their values in this way they do not always converge on the same result. That, according to moral relativism, is what accounts for persistent basic moral disagreement.

Furthermore, relativists deny that the persistence of such basic moral disagreement is due simply to some people being better placed to discover the moral truth, the absolutist explanation of the persistence of disagreement. To a relativist, that is like saying that people in one particular spatio-temporal framework are better placed than other people are to discover what the objectively correct spatio-temporal framework is.

1.4 Evaluative Relativity: "Good For"

We might compare the relativity of moral wrongness with the way in which something that is good for one person may not be good for another person. If Tom has bet on a horse that runs well in the rain and Sue has bet on a horse that does not run well in the rain, then rain is good for Tom and bad for Sue. This is an uncontroversial example of evaluative relativity. The rain is good in relation to Tom's goals and bad in relation to Sue's.

Similarly, abortion can be immoral with respect to (the moral coordinates determined by) Tom's values and not immoral with respect to Sue's. Moral relativists sometimes express this by saying that abortion is immoral "for Tom" and not immoral "for Sue." Of course, what is meant here is not that abortion is bad for Tom but not bad for Sue in the sense of harmful to one but not the other, nor is it just to say that Tom may think abortion immoral and Sue may think it moral. The rain might be good for Tom even if he doesn't realize it and abortion might be immoral for Tom whether or not he realizes that it is.

Notice, by the way, that a speaker does not always have to make explicit for whom a given situation is good. In particular, if Max has bet on the same horse as Alice and he is speaking to Alice, out of the hearing of Sue, he can say simply. "This rain is bad," meaning that it is bad for him and Alice.

Similarly, a moral relativist talking to another moral relativist can suppress reference to a particular set of values if the judgment is supposed to hold in relation both to the (moral coordinates determined by the) values accepted by the speaker and to the (moral coordinates determined by the) values accepted by the hearer. If Sue and Arthur both have values with the same implications for abortion, and Tom isn't listening, Sue might say simply, "Abortion is not morally wrong", meaning that it is not wrong in relation to her and Arthur's values. It is not wrong for either of them.

In saying, "This rain is bad," Tom means (roughly) that it is bad for himself and his audience; not just that it is bad for himself. The remark, "This rain is bad" is not normally equivalent to "This rain is bad for me." When Tom tells someone else that the rain is bad, he means (roughly) that it is bad in relation to certain goals, purposes, aims, or values that he takes himself to share with his audience. If Mary knows that Tom has bet on a horse that runs well in the rain and she has bet on a horse that does not run well in the rain, it would normally be misleading for her to tell Tom, simply, "This rain is bad." Such a remark would be overly self-centered. In the absence of some more or less clearly indicated qualification, evaluative remarks are understood as having been made from a point of view that is presumed to be shared by speaker and audience. If Mary is only talking about herself, she should make that explicit and say, "This rain is bad for me."

Notice that the rain can bad for a group of people without being bad for each of them taken individually. It might be bad for them taken collectively. If the other school's football team plays better in the rain, "This rain is bad" might mean "this rain is bad for our side." (Similarly, the values of a group might not be the values of any individual in the group (Gilbert, 1989).)

Thomson (1992, 1994) takes the remark, "This rain is bad," to be "incomplete." That seems right. However, in the present instance we cannot simply equate the remark, "This rain is bad," with the more complete remark, "This rain is bad for us." There is a subtle difference. To see the difference, consider a situation in which Mary has bet on a horse that does not run well in the rain and she thinks, incorrectly, that Tom has also bet on that horse. Suppose Tom has bet on the horse that runs well in the rain, but Mary does not realize this. If in this context she says to Tom, "This rain is bad for us," then it is clear how to evaluate her remark. What she says is simply false, since it is not the case that the rain is bad for both of them. But if instead she were to say to Tom, "This rain is bad," then it is far from clear that what she says is false. Her remark to Tom presupposes shared interests or outlook. If that presupposition is incorrect, we do not normally try to assign truth or falsity to her remark. So in certain circumstances there is a difference between. "This rain is bad" and "This rain is bad for us."

Similarly, suppose the moral relativist, Sue, thinking she and Tom have relevantly similar standards, says to him, "abortion is morally permissible," suppressing mention of standards. Sue's remark is not to be treated as false merely because she is wrong in supposing she and Tom share principles that permit abortion.

1.5 Relativity Theory

Something that is good for some people is bad for others, indifferent to yet others. Moral relativism says that the same is true of moral values and moral norms. According to moral relativism whether something is morally good, right, or just is always relative to a set of moral coordinates, a set of values or moral standards, a certain moral point of view.

Moral relativism holds that there are various sets of moral coordinates or moral outlooks with different standards of right and wrong. People's values differ with respect to the relative weight given to liberty versus equality, and to general welfare versus the development of art and science. They also differ with respect to the extent of the moral community: some restrict it to family and friends; others include all people of a certain race or caste or country; some include all people of whatever race or class; others count animals and even plants as part of the moral community to be protected by the moral rules.

To repeat our earlier "first approximation," moral relativism makes the following claim about moral judgments:

> For the purposes of assigning truth conditions, a judgment of the form, it would be morally wrong of P to D, has to be understood as elliptical for a judgment of the form, in relation to moral framework M, it would be morally wrong of P to D. Similarly for other moral judgments.

Recall that moral relativism is not by itself a claim about meaning. It does not say that speakers always *intend* their moral judgments to be relational in this respect. It is clear that many speakers do not. Moral relativism is a thesis about how things are and a thesis about how things aren't! Moral relativism claims that there is no such thing as objectively absolute good, absolute right, or absolute justice; there is only what is good, right, or just in relation to this or that moral framework. What someone takes to be absolute rightness is only rightness in relation to (a system of moral coordinates determined by) that person's values.

Earlier, I compared moral relativism with Einstein's theory of relativity in physics, which says that physical magnitudes, like mass, length, or temporal duration, are relative to a frame of reference, so that two events that are simultaneous with respect to one frame of reference can fail to be simultaneous with respect to another. In saying this, Einstein's theory does not make a claim about speakers' intentions. It does not claim that speakers intend to be making relational judgments when they speak of mass or simultaneity. The claim is, rather, that there is no such thing as absolute simultaneity or absolute mass. There is only simultaneity or mass with respect to one or another frame of reference. What someone might take to be absolute magnitudes are really relative magnitudes: magnitudes that are relative to that person's frame of reference.

Imagine a difference of opinion about whether event E precedes event F. According to Einstein's theory of relativity, there may be no uniform answer to this question: perhaps, in relation to one framework E precedes F, while in relation to a different framework E does not precede F.

Similarly, consider a moral disagreement about whether we are right to raise animals for food. Moral relativism holds that there is no uniform answer to this question: in relation to (the system of moral coordinates determined by) one person's values it is permissible to raise animals for food and in relation to (the system of moral coordinates determined by) a different person's values it is not permissible to raise animals for food. To repeat: what someone takes to be absolute rightness is only rightness in relation to (a system of moral coordinates determined by) that person's values.

Moral relativism does not claim that moral differences by themselves entail moral relativism, any more than Einstein claimed that differences in opinion about simultaneity by themselves entailed relativistic physics. We have to consider what differences there are or could be and why this might be so. How are we to explain the sorts of moral differences that actually occur? Can we seriously suppose that there is an answer to the question about the justice of our treatment of animals that is independent of one or another moral framework? What is the best explanation of differences in this and other areas of seeming intractability?

I emphasize again that moral relativism does not identify what is right in relation to a given moral framework with whatever is taken to be right by those who accept that framework. That would be like saying Einstein's theory of relativity treats two events as simultaneous with respect to a given coordinate system if people at rest with respect to the coordinate system believe the events are simultaneous.

2

Social Contracts

2.1 Resolving Moral Disputes

Consider the following objection to moral relativism.

Objection: It is a bad strategy to take moral relativism seriously. We should always assume that our moral differences can be resolved by reviewing the evidence, gathering more evidence, and considering what conclusion is best supported by this evidence; otherwise, we miss an opportunity to resolve our disputes. If we decide a dispute is not rationally resolvable in this way, we will stop trying to resolve it, and, if we are wrong and the dispute could have been rationally resolvable, e.g., through the consideration of more evidence, we will have missed an opportunity to resolve it.

Two responses can be made to this objection. First it overlooks the cost of wrongly thinking a dispute is rationally resolvable when it is not rationally resolvable. The policy suggested in the objection can lead to pointless argument. Second, and more important, the policy suggested can also lead one to overlook other reasonable ways to resolve moral disputes, ways that go beyond trying to reach conclusions on the basis of evidence.

People care about what they value. A vegetarian wants to get people to stop raising animals for food. The anti-abortionist wants to get others to end the practice of abortion. Moral differences involve conflicts in affective attitude that are resolved only if agreement is reached on what to do.

Affective attitudes are attitudes with "affect," that is, feeling, impulse, motivation, and caring. Such attitudes include hope, desire, wishing, fear, and hatred. Affective attitudes contrast with cognitive attitudes like belief, expectation, perception, and doubt. Of course, many attitudes are both affective and cognitive. To be happy that something is so includes having the cognitive attitude that it is so and an affective attitude of happiness. And belief in someone may be as much an affective as a cognitive attitude.

Conflicts in affective attitude do not have to involve conflicts in belief. Suppose the Reds and the Greens are two competing football teams, Alice favors the Reds, and Bertie favors the Greens. What's good for Alice's side is not what's good for Bertie's and they can agree about that. When Alice says to herself or her teammates, "This rain is bad" (because the Reds do not play well in the rain), and Bertie says to himself or his teammates, "This rain is good" (because the Greens do play well in the rain), they are not contradicting each other but there is still a clash of affective attitudes. Bertie is happy about the rain and Alice is unhappy about it.

Similar differences in affective attitude occur when people have different values, with the additional feature that people may try to convert others to their own values. Whereas Alice does not try to convert Bertie to her side, some vegetarians try to get others to become vegetarians in order to advance vegetarian goals.

A related type of difference in affective attitude occurs in bargaining (Stevenson, 1963a). Someone selling a house wants to sell it for a higher price, a potential purchaser wants to buy the house for a lower price. They must bargain to reach agreement on what the price will be.

Similarly, labor wants a higher wage rate, management wants a lower rate. Their difference is resolved when an agreement is reached at what the wage rate is to be. The parties to the bargaining then come to accept a practical arrangement: they will adhere to a certain set of principles relating work and pay.

When people bargain about a wage rate or about the price of a house, they do not just try to show that a certain outcome is the one objectively supported by the evidence, given acceptable general principles. They also make and accept various proposals and the outcome is influenced by the bargaining power of the participants.

Political and moral disputes often involve bargaining. We argue with others, not only by showing how features of their moral frameworks should lead them in certain directions in the light of the facts; we also give them practical reasons to modify their moral understandings. "If you don't do this, we won't do that." Disadvantaged groups can threaten to withhold full participation in a moral framework unless their disadvantage is lessened or removed.

This complicates the question whether we ought to assume moral disputes are always rationally resolvable. It depends on what counts as a "rational resolution" of a moral dispute. If moral bargaining is included, then it may indeed be useful to assume (until proven otherwise) that a moral dispute is rationally resolvable.

2.2 Conventions

It is likely that most people's values reflect conventions that are maintained by continual tacit bargaining and adjustment. Hume (1739) observes that two people rowing a boat continually adjust their rates of rowing so that they come to row at the same rate, a rate that is normally somewhere between the rate at which each would prefer to row. In the same way the basic values accepted by people of different powers and resources are the result of a continually changing compromise affecting such things as the relative importance attached to helping others as compared with the importance attached to not harming others.

2.3 Moral Conventions

We can imagine conventions developing from scratch in the way that people might arrive at a rate of rowing from scratch. Mary doesn't push Jack around on condition that Jack does not push her around. She is nice to him so that he will be nice to her. The two of them adopt a value of respecting the other as a useful convention. Living together, they reach an arrangement about who will take care of what household duties: for example, she washes the dishes and he dries them; she sweeps the floor and he takes out the garbage.

The relevant conventions may or may not be arrived at openly and explicitly. There may be a specific agreement, "I'll do the floors; you take out the garbage." Or they may just fall into a pattern without discussion.

Any association of friends has its conventional understandings. In an open society, these may be quite fragile. If one finds that one is not getting all one hoped for from an arrangement, or one finds that one is not happy even getting all one hoped for, one may be able to drop these friends and go on to others. In some situations, however, it is difficult simply to opt out of ongoing arrangements, especially where the arrangements are widely accepted in society.

Social contract theories of morality (Gauthier, 1986; Hardin, 1988) envision the whole of morality and politics as arising in this way from conventions adopted for self-interested reasons. A custom of truth-telling arises because it is useful to be able to get information from others and others will tell the truth to you only if you make a practice of telling the truth to you. Promises are kept for a similar reason. An institution of property arises as people see its advantages, etc.

Once a body of conventional morality has been established, it becomes relatively difficult to modify. There is social pressure not to violate the conventional principles, including social penalties for such violation. But changes can and will occur.

Some people will violate conventional morality if it is to their advantage to do so and they can get away from it. People who are relatively disadvantaged by conventional morality may try to renegotiate a more favorable outcome.

Significant renegotiation must occur in the political realm. Political movements are formed around social issues. Moral argument becomes political argument, including ordinary party politics, public protests, disruptions, and even violence.

2.3.1 Harming Versus Not Helping

One can begin to appreciate the conventional self-interested source of principles of morality by considering certain aspects of ordinary moral views. For example, most people take the duty not to initiate harm to others to be much stricter than the duty to help others avoid the same sort of harm (Foot, 1978e).[1] So, for example, most people suppose that it is worse to kill several people (for example, by sending them poisoned chocolates) than to fail to save several people from death (for example, by not sending them food that would keep them from starving). And most people think that it is not morally permissible to kill a healthy hospital visitor even if the visitor's organs were then used to save several people who would otherwise die.

From a utilitarian point of view, this may seem puzzling, because the same utility is lost when one fails to help someone avoid harm as when one initiates the harm oneself. And, although there have been many ingenious attempts to try to give a utilitarian rationale for the different strengths of these duties, none of these attempts has been successful in my opinion (Harman, 1980).

I suggest that the difference in strictness we attach to these duties is a consequence of the fact that morality represents a compromise between people of different powers and resources. Everyone benefits from a strict duty not to harm others, but only the poor would benefit from an equally strict duty to help

---

[1] Many people recognize an exception when runaway trolleys and similar phenomena are involved, although it is not easy to say what the relevant similarity is or why there should be such an exception. Thomson (1986, 1990) discusses some of the complexities.

others avoid harm. Wealthy people would not benefit from a strict duty of mutual aid because, given their resources, they would be called upon to do most of the helping and would have little need for such help for themselves. Wealthy people would benefit from a strict duty not to harm others, however, since they could be harmed if poor people were to organize against them. Therefore, although everyone will be in favor of a strict duty not to initiate harm against others, an equally strict duty of mutual aid will be favored only by poor people and not by wealthy people. If, as I suggest, our moral principles represent a compromise between richer and poorer people that would explain why our morality contains a strict principle of noninjury and a somewhat weaker principle of mutual aid, the exact relative strengths of each depending on the relative bargaining positions of rich versus poor.

2.3.2 Treatment of Animals

Eventually I want to consider whether an explanation in terms of relative bargaining positions might undercut the normative force of the distinction we make between harming and not helping. But before I get to that, let me go back to the difference in the way we think we should behave toward animals and toward people. Although most people feel that some ways of treating animals are wrong, most people also believe that the moral limits on behavior toward animals are quite different from the moral limits on behavior toward people. Most people see nothing wrong with the ways in which animals are kept as pets, raised as food, hunted for sport, and used for medical experiments, although they would think it wrong to treat people in this way. From a utilitarian point of view, there is little justification for this difference. Animals are sentient beings with their own lives to lead. Why should they be given such an inferior status as compared with people (Singer, 1975)?

It is easy to explain the difference in moral status of people and animals if we suppose this has its source in conventions we accept for mainly self-interested reasons. Our moral conventions favor people over animals because they are conventions arrived at by people for people. The animals do not participate. If at a given time morality discriminates against some part of society, the affected people can try to put pressure on the others to change this part of morality. They can threaten to withhold their own participation in the moral conventions. This can lead to changes in the morality. But the animals cannot get together to put pressure on people in the same way.

A convention theory of morality has no problem explaining why animals have a lower moral status than people do. If there is a problem, it is the opposite one of explaining why animals have any moral status at all in our morality. What explains our moral disapproval of cruelty to animals, given that animals do not participate in our conventions?

We could instead say that this is connected with our caring about animals, with our having some sympathy with them. But then the explanatory work is being done by the assumption about what people care about and not by the assumption that justice is conventional. If we had to explain moral conventions for dealing with people by invoking the assumption that people care about other people, convention would not play as major a role in morality as (I believe) it does.

2.4 Explaining Concern for Others

There is clearly some connection between morality and concern and respect for others. One possible view is that we are genetically constructed so as to feel such concern and respect for others and that makes morality possible (Hamilton, 1964; Trivers, 1971).

There may well be something to this sociobiological thesis; but there may also be a completely conventional explanation of our concern for others. Perhaps one develops concern and respect for others as part of accepting a convention, on the supposition that others are developing or have developed similar concern and respect. Such concern and respect might be developed through practice. One develops a habit of taking an interest in others. This is possible because taking an interest in something or someone is the kind of thing one can do. One watches a game on television and decides to root for one or another of the teams; one does this to make the game more interesting to watch; doing so structures one's perception of the game. Similarly, one takes an interest in a conversation at a party because that makes it less boring to stand there and listen. In playing a game with friends, one takes an interest in winning; otherwise one's friends will get mad. In the same way, one might take an interest in the welfare of other people. This is something one is encouraged to do as a child and one can develop the habit of doing it.

If a conventional explanation of concern and respect is correct, one would initially tend to feel concern and respect only for certain selected people, those who participate in the relevant conventions, which at first are the practices of one's family and later are the practices of those one comes into contact with. Stimulus generalization then occur. Given a disposition to feel concern and respect for certain people, there will be a tendency for the disposition to apply to similar cases, so one may find oneself with concern and respect for outsiders, too. One might even come through stimulus generalization to be disposed to feel a certain concern for animals. In this way, the theory that morality is conventional might be part of the explanation of our positive feelings about animals.

This is highly speculative, of course – just a possibility.

2.5 Do the Explanations Undermine the Principles Explained?

One possible reaction to an explanation of moral views in terms of bargaining position and power relationships is to think that the explanation actually *undermines* the views by showing that they are based on morally irrelevant considerations.

Two different reasons might lie behind this reaction. First, it might be thought that morality loses its normative force if it does not have a nonconventional source. But that is just a mistake if moral conventionalism is true. According to moral conventionalism, morality must be seen as lacking any objective absolute normative force, of course, because according to moral conventionalism there is no such thing as objective absolute normative force. Morality does not lose that sort of normative force, because it never had it in the first place. And morality will continue to have its relative normative force, just as it always has.

Second, it might be thought there is something unjust about agreements whose outcome is affected by the differences in power relationships among the affected parties. It may not seem fair that poor people should have to accept only limited help from wealthy people simply because of the bargaining strength of wealthy people. It may not seem fair that animals should be placed in an inferior moral status simply because they are not able to participate in the bargaining that leads to the relevant moral conventions. This is the worry I want to consider now.

What is the source of these moral judgments about unfairness? If moral conventionalism is correct, these judgments must be based ultimately on values that are part of the conventional morality accepted by those who make the judgments.

If so, there may be a tension or instability between certain moral views and an explanation of those views in terms of differences in bargaining position. The tension could be resolved if we could give up the explanation, but I see no other plausible way to explain the moral distinction we make between harming and not helping, or the differences in treatment we feel are appropriate toward animals and people. Suppose, then, that we cannot give up these explanations. How else might the tension be resolved?

One possibility would be simply to conclude that the relevant agreements are completely null and void. That would presumably mean that people have no moral reason to adhere to the agreements. It might mean that there is no reason to refrain from harming other people. That would be a disastrous result!

There are two less disastrous possibilities. First, one might give up the idea that there is anything unfair about the agreement. Second, one might give up the idea that unfair agreements are completely null and void, at least when they are basic moral agreements. One might concede that the unfairness of the agreement provides some reason to try modify the results of the agreement so that they come to be more in accord with what might have emerged if the bargaining position of affected parties had been the same.

Those with a superior bargaining position will be attracted by the first possibility, namely, giving up the idea that the agreement is unfair. Those with an inferior bargaining position will be attracted by the second suggestion to retain the idea that the agreement is unfair and take this as a reason to make the outcome fairer.

Would either side have an advantage? It might be said that those who want to modify the agreement have a bit of an edge, since they are simply drawing a consequence from the principles that have been accepted in the past by all in the relevant group. But the other side can say with equal justice that they too are simply drawing a consequence from principles accepted in the past by all in the relevant group, since the accepted principles have involved taking harming to be more seriously wrong than not helping, and have taken animals to have an inferior moral status to humans. When there is a tension or inconsistency in a set of accepted moral principles, given certain factual assumptions, conflicting positions can be derived. The resulting dispute can only be resolved when some new, consistent consensus is reached.

In fact, most people do not seem to think that vast differences in power by themselves make an agreement invalid. For example, it is widely thought that contracts made by individuals with large banks and other corporations are often legally and morally binding, despite extreme differences in bargaining power of those involved. So it is possible that there is no real problem here.

2.6 Moral Argument

Moral argument often involves consideration of how previously accepted principles apply to new cases, as well as the way in which various moral judgments might be accommodated by appeal to newly-stated principles. It also happens that some people advocate new principles and new interpretations of old principles out of a concern for their own self-interest. This is often thought to be quite disreputable, but I am saying we ought to count it as a perfectly acceptable form of moral argument.

Moral bargaining is often potentially involved in moral argument because there is often a possibility that those dissatisfied with the outcome will refuse to continue to play their role under an old consensus, will turn the issue into a political issue, will organize strikes and other forms of protest, or in the extreme will go into active rebellion. To the extent that others have a reason to avoid such developments, they have a reason to accept the suggested reinterpretation of the principles involved.

Often what looks like a simple dispute as to the implications of previously accepted moral principles is really an instance of this sort of moral bargaining. Members of disadvantaged groups argue that considerations of fairness support certain conclusions, even if these considerations have not been previously understood as supporting those conclusions. Conservatives reject this sort of argument. I suggest that in such a case the disadvantaged people are usefully interpreted as expressing dissatisfaction with the current consensus, and are threatening to withdraw support unless this consensus is modified in certain ways. The conservatives are threatening not to go along with any such change, and are invoking worries about what it would be like to abandon any sort of moral consensus altogether.

Recent changes in conventional sexual morality seem clearly to have been affected by moral bargaining. Changes in what counts as politeness between men and women were effected when many women began to object to having men open doors for them or hold their chairs for them. Active protests and demonstrations have led to changes in what counts as "assent" to sexual intercourse and so what counts as "rape" or "sexual assault."

Self-interest is not the only factor that can fuel such disputes. This emerges in the argument over abortion. Self-interest plays a part in that argument, namely the self-interest of those who see themselves as benefiting from women having the right to abortion. But prior principle is what is most important on the other side. Indeed, prior principle almost always plays an important role in a moral dispute and not just as a peg on which to hang one's self-interested claims.

3
Expressing Basic Disagreement

3.1 The "Emotive Use" of Language

People who accept different moral frameworks typically have conflicting affective attitudes. One person may wish to end the practice of raising animals for food, another may be in favor of that practice. In some sense, they disagree with each other, but moral relativism does not appear to provide them with any easy way to express their disagreement. Each agrees that raising animals for food is wrong relative to the first moral framework, and that raising animals for food is not wrong relative to the second.

How can moral relativists use language to express disagreements they take to be fundamental? How should Veronica, a committed vegetarian, express her disagreement with Archie, a committed nonvegetarian?

Veronica can say that she and Archie disagree over what the rules are to be for the treatment of animals, just as two people bargaining over the price of a house can say they disagree over what the price of the house is to be, where that is not a disagreement over what the price of the house *ought* to be. Moral relativists who disagree about sexual morality or economic fairness can similarly engage in moral bargaining without supposing that they are bargaining over what the rules morally ought to be in some nonrelativistic sense of "morally ought."

Emotivists (Ayer, 1946; Stevenson, 1963a) argue against restricting moral terminology in the relativistic way and in favor of using moral terminology to express affective attitudes. In its crudest form, emotivism offers a "Boo! Hurrah! Who cares!" account of the meaning of moral discourse. "It is morally wrong to eat meat" means something like "Boo to meat eating!" and "Eating meat is not wrong" means something like "Eating meat, who cares?"

Somewhat more sophisticated versions of emotivism (Hare, 1952) treat moral judgments as imperatives: "Don't ever eat meat!" versus "Eat meat if you want to!" All these views differ from moral relativism in allowing moral judgments that do not have a truth value. "Boo to meet eating!" and "Don't eat meat!" are neither true nor false.

Emotivism, unlike pure moral relativism, allows people with different moral frameworks to express moral disagreements. On the other hand, the crudest forms of emotivism allow only the simplest forms of moral judgment, not permitting more complex judgments, like:

(1) It is morally wrong to encourage someone to do something that is morally wrong.

It is not easy to see what affective attitude or imperative could be expressed by the second occurrence of the phrase *morally wrong in* (1). And neither of the following remarks is very good English:

(2) Boo to encouraging someone to do something that boo to it!

(3) Don't ever encourage someone to do something that don't ever do!

3.2 Quasi-Absolutism

Hare (1952) extends his imperative analysis to include more complex judgments. He assumes a "use theory of meaning," which holds that the meaning of an expression is explained to the extent that its use is explained, where an important part of use has to do with what remarks one takes to be implied by or to contradict other remarks.

In this view, to accept a simple general imperative is (a) to intend to follow it oneself and (b) to favor other people following it. Acceptance of more complex judgments involves having dispositions to accept simple general imperatives under certain conditions, dispositions that are reflected in a "logic of imperatives." For example, acceptance of (3) amounts to being prepared to accept an implication from any general imperative of the form,

(1) Don't ever F.

to the corresponding imperative of the form,

(2) Don't ever encourage someone to F.

Roughly speaking, that amounts to being disposed to accept something of the form, (2) whenever one accepts something of the form (1).

If Hare's approach works out, it is possible to appeal only to ingredients that are acceptable to a moral relativist in order to construct a way of using moral terminology that mimics the absolutist usage. In other words, Hare's view is a form of what I will call "quasi-absolutism." Such a view is sometimes called "projectivism" or "quasi-realism" (Blackburn, 1993a, b).

In perhaps the simplest form of quasi-absolutism, a moral relativist projects his or her moral framework onto the world and then uses moral terminology as if the projected morality were the single true morality, while at the same time admitting that this way of talking is only "as if." The supposed advantage of this quasi-absolutist usage is that it allows people with different moral frameworks to disagree with each other. (Critics of the proposal might claim that it only allows such people to appear to disagree with each other!)

The central assumption behind quasi-absolutism is that words can be given meaning by being given a use. If we sufficiently specify how moral terminology is to be used, we have given it a meaning. If we can give a full characterization of this usage appealing only to assumptions acceptable to moral relativism, then we can use words as the absolutist does without having to accept moral absolutism. We may be able to have our cake and eat it too!

I do not know whether the central assumption about meaning and use is correct. (I discuss that assumption in Harman, 1987, 1990, 1993a, 1993b). If the central assumption is correct, then quasi-absolutism is plausible and, as we shall see, a problem arises about the correct statement of moral relativism. In order to explore that problem, I will for the rest of this chapter accept the central assumption about meaning and use.

I now want to say more about how quasi-absolutism might be developed. In order to avoid equivocation, I will use all capital letters to mark the quasi-absolutist use of moral terminology. Then, we are to imagine that Veronica and Archie express their disagreement as follows: Veronica says that it is WRONG to raise animals for food and Archie says that it is not WRONG to do so. I will call moral terms "QA terms" when they are used in this way.

Following Hare (1952) and Wong (1984) I will suppose that QA terms are used to express the speaker's attitude toward certain standards. For example, in saying that raising animals for food is WRONG, Veronica expresses her approval of moral standards that would prohibit the practice. In saying that raising animals for food is not WRONG, Archie expresses approval of standards that do not prohibit raising animals for food.

Expressing an attitude is different from talking about it. When Veronica expresses her approval of moral standards that prohibit raising animals for food, she does not talk about her approval any more than she talks about her belief that cats are animals when she expresses that belief.

Archie can disagree with a belief of Veronica's without disagreeing with the claim that she has it. Similarly, he can disagree in attitude with her about raising animals for food without denying that she has the attitude she has.

Now, this use of QA terminology to express a speaker's attitudes is not supposed to be its only use. QA words are not used merely to blurt out a speaker's attitudes or emotions. Indeed, at least four other features characterize the use of the expression *WRONG*.

First, that expression can be used in all contexts in which the term *morally wrong* would normally be used in English.

Second, at any given moment, a speaker who uses the term *WRONG* will normally be willing to say something using that term if and only if he or she is willing to assert the corresponding thing with the word *wrong* replacing *WRONG*, using the word *wrong* in relation to the relevant morality associated with his or her own values. As we shall see in a moment this is supposed to hold only for so-called "extensional contexts" as opposed to contexts of direct or indirect quotation, propositional attitude, or modality.

It follows that a moral relativist who also uses QA terminology should accept

(3) *X* is *WRONG* if and only if *X* is wrong in relation to the morality relevantly associated with my current values.

(3) follows by the preceding principle given that the speaker asserts the tautology, "X is wrong in relation to the morality relevantly associated with my current values if and only if X is wrong in relation to the morality associated with my current values." [Replace the first occurrence of the phrase "wrong in relation to my current values" with "WRONG."]

Here it is important to recall that what is wrong in relation to the morality relevantly associated with a particular person's values is not to be identified with what the person currently *thinks* is wrong in relation to his or her values. So, even though a speaker maintains the above principle, the speaker should not maintain, "*X* is WRONG if and only if I think that *X* is wrong in relation to the morality relevantly associated with my values."

Despite the fact that a speaker will accept the displayed principle, the expression *WRONG* is not supposed to be synonymous with "morally wrong in relation to the morality relevantly associated with my current values."

Indeed, a third further feature of the supposed use of this expression is that, even though Veronica is a moral relativist, she is supposed to be able to describe her disagreement with

Archie as a disagreement about whether raising animals for food is WRONG and Archie, another moral relativist, is supposed to be able agree with her description of their disagreement. But neither Veronica nor Archie supposes that they disagree about whether raising animals for food is prohibited by Veronica's values! They both agree that it is prohibited by those values. Their disagreement concerns which values are to be adopted.

Notice that Veronica can assert, "Archie and I do not disagree about whether raising animals for food is wrong in relation to my values," without being willing to maintain what results when "WRONG" is substituted in her assertion for "wrong in relation to my values," yielding, "Archie and I do not disagree about whether raising animals for food is WRONG." The fact that she does not accept this replacement for her original remark does not violate the second point just mentioned, because the context is one of indirect quotation or propositional attitude. It talks in part about what Archie and she *disagree* about.

A fourth feature of the supposed usage is that speaker's who use the QA terminology should recognize standard logical implications among remarks using that terminology. Consider the following remarks:

(4) It is WRONG to encourage someone to do something WRONG.

(5) Raising animals for food is WRONG.

(6) It is WRONG to encourage someone to raise animals for food.

Veronica and Archie agree about (4), because each believes with respect to his or her (different) values V that it is wrong in relation to V to encourage someone to do something that is wrong in relation to V. Both Veronica and Archie take (4) and (5) to imply (6), although of course only Veronica accepts (5) and so (6).

These four features taken together would seem to provide a moral relativist with sufficient instruction for using QA terminology in many contexts.

3.3 Truth

The fourth point, about implication, may seem to cast doubt on the intelligibility of quasi-absolutism. It would seem that, if Veronica uses the word *WRONG* in such a way that such implications hold, she is committed to supposing that such remarks are susceptible of being true or false, because to suppose that (4) and (5) imply (6) is to suppose that (6) is true whenever (4) and (5) are true. But can she coherently suppose that statements like (4), (5), and (6) can be true or false?

Indeed, what truth conditions could there be for (5), "Raising animals for food is WRONG"? If Veronica tries to explain the truth conditions in terms of the relativistic notion of *wrong*, it seems that she must suppose that (5) is true if and only if raising animals for food is wrong in relation to her values *V*, whereas Archie holds that (5) is true if and only if raising animals for food is wrong in relation to his values *W*, where *V* and *W* are quite different. But if Veronica and Archie assign different truth conditions to (5), they do not mean the same thing by it.

Quasi-absolutists can reply that this objection has an easy and somewhat trivial answer. The truth conditions that Veronica and Archie assign in common to (5) have to be stated using the expression *WRONG*, not the relativistic term *wrong* (Stevenson, 1963, pp. 214–20; Stoljar, 1993). Veronica and Archie both suppose that (5) is true, if, and only if, raising animals for food is WRONG.

It must be conceded that the trivial answer about truth conditions is sufficient for purposes of saying (a) how Veronica and Archie can assign the same truth conditions to claims involving expressions like *WRONG* and (b) how there can be implications among claims involving QA terms. Because of its triviality, it is not a very substantial account of truth conditions, but a more substantial account appears not to be needed for these purposes.[1]

---

[1] Horwich (1990) argues that this sort of trivial account is suitable for all purposes.

3.4 Defining Moral Relativism

At this point we need to go reconsider our initial definition of moral relativism (2), which I renumber here.

(1) For the purposes of assigning truth conditions, a judgment of the form, *it would be morally wrong of P to D*, has to be understood as elliptical for a judgment of the form, *in relation to moral framework M, it would be morally wrong of P to D*. Similarly for other moral judgments.

The trouble with this is that if quasi-absolutism is correct, a moral relativist must acknowledge that an ordinary judgment of the form, *it would be morally wrong of P to D*, can be equated with *it would be morally WRONG of P to D*. Truth conditions can then be assigned of the trivial sort just mentioned. So, (1) is false, given quasi-absolutism.

We might try the following definition:

(2) For the purposes of assigning truth conditions, a judgment of the form, *it would be morally wrong of P to D*, has to be understood, either as elliptical for a judgment of the form, *in relation to moral framework M, it would be morally wrong of P to D*, or as equivalent to *it would be morally WRONG of P to D*. Similarly for other moral judgments.

But (2) by itself leaves a couple of loose ends. First, (2) is complicated in an ad hoc way. Second, and more importantly, (2) does not obviously exclude moral absolutism, because (a) quasi-absolutism assumes that meaning is determined by usage and (b) the usage of QA terms is deliberately designed to mimic the usage of the corresponding absolutist terms! It looks as if the absolutist terminology is going to count as QA terminology, just going by usage.

Recall the features of QA terminology mentioned so far. First, the terminology has to be usable to express disagreements in attitude about moral standards. Clearly, the moral absolutist uses his or her terminology in that way. Second, a QA term like *WRONG* can be used in all contexts in which the term *morally wrong* would normally be used in English. The absolutist's use of morally wrong trivially satisfies that condition. Third, a speaker should normally be willing to use a term like *WRONG* if and only if he on she is willing to make the corresponding statement using the phrase *wrong in relation to the relevant morality associated with my values*. Since the absolutist believes that the relevant morality is always the same, no matter what a person's values, the absolutist's usage of *morally wrong* coincides with *morally WRONG* with respect to this feature, too. Finally, a speaker should treat remarks with QA terminology as susceptible of the sorts of logical implications normally associated with remarks using the corresponding moral terminology. Clearly, the absolutist's moral terminology satisfies this condition.

If we are to use something like (2) to define moral relativism, we need to find some other way to distinguish the relativist's use of the QA terminology from the absolutist's moral terminology.

Now, where do the relativist and the absolutist differ? They differ with respect to their understanding of certain sorts of persisting moral disagreements. The absolutist supposes that moral disagreements occur either as a result of some participants making mistakes about the situation, or reasoning badly, or simply because some participants are better placed than others to arrive at the truth. The relativist supposes that many such disagreements do not rest on mistakes of fact or reasoning or the fact that some participants are simply not well placed to arrive at the truth. That is, the relativist supposes that the situation is similar to the situation with respect to motion, simultaneity, and mass.

It would be natural to try to express this difference by saying that the absolutist, but not the relativist, thinks that the moral disputes in question have answers in the sense that, apart from borderline cases, one disputant is right and the other mistaken. But the use of QA terminology would allow the relativist to say this also: one disputant is right about what is WRONG, the other is mistaken.

It might be said that the difference then has to do with whether these "truths" are factual. The relativist does not think that there are nonrelative facts corresponding to truths expressed using *WRONG* and other moral QA terminology The relativist supposes that the only factual moral truths are relational truths, such as that something is wrong in relation to one or another set of standards. The absolutist thinks there are nonrelative moral facts.

However, a sophisticated quasi-absolutism can allow for nonrelative moral "facts" corresponding to statements using QA terminology in exactly the same way that it allows for "truths," holding that it is a fact that raising animals for food is WRONG if and only if raising animals for food is WRONG.

3.4.1 Objective Truth Conditions

I suggest we express the difference between relativism and absolutism like this: the relativist does not suppose that the "truth conditions" for statements using QA terminology are *objective* truth conditions, in a sense of *objective* which I will now try to explain; the absolutist supposes that the truth conditions for ordinary nonrelative moral statements are objective. The relativist holds that there are no objective nonrelative facts about moral right and wrong; the absolutist says that there are objective nonrelative facts about moral right and wrong.

Although I cannot offer a strict definition of the relevant sense of *objective*, I will try to explain the relevant sort of objectivity with reference to relativism about motion.

A relativist about motion supposes that there are various possible spatio-temporal frameworks, none of which is objectively privileged, even though one might be specially salient to a given observer, for example, the framework in which that observer is at rest (or the framework in which the Earth is at rest, or the solar system . . .). The moral relativist supposes that there are various moral frameworks from which moral issues can be judged and that none of these frameworks is objectively privileged, even though one might be specially salient to a given person: for example, the moral framework relevantly associated with that person's values.

If the relativist uses the QA terminology to say, e.g., that raising animals for food is WRONG, the relativist may suppose that the remark has "truth" conditions, and indeed, is "true." But the relativist also must suppose that the truth conditions of this remark are subjective rather than objective. If the relativist thought these were the objective truth conditions, and that the remark was objectively true, the relativist would be committed to thinking that there was after all a morality that was objectively privileged.

In attempting to respond to moral relativism, it is clearly not enough to say that a particular moral framework is privileged in the sense that it is the one that correctly captures what is RIGHT and WRONG. That would be like responding to relativism about motion by claiming that a certain spatio-temporal framework is privileged in the sense that it is the one that correctly captures when things are really in motion and when they are not. If there is no way to determine which framework is privileged in the relevant sense, then we must ask whether there is any reason to think there is such a privileged framework.

We can envision a quasi-absolutist use of terms to express opinions about absolute motion, by analogy with the QA terminology. To say that something was in MOTION would be a way of expressing one's views about its motion in relation to the most salient spatio-temporal framework and to express one's "disagreement" with other people to whom different spati-temporal frameworks are more salient. The mere availability of such a way of talking could have no relevance to the issue of the relativity of motion. It would not provide a way to defend absolute space and time. One could not reasonably say, using that terminology, that a certain spatio-temporal framework is indeed objectively privileged in correctly capturing whether things are in MOTION.

Similarly, one cannot adequately respond to the arguments for moral relativism simply by saying that there *is* a privileged moral framework, namely, that framework that correctly captures whether things are RIGHT and WRONG. One needs to show that there is an objectively privileged framework, one that is not just a "projection" of the QA terminology.

This suggests that we can replace our earlier definitions of moral relativism with:

(3) For the purposes of assigning *objective* truth conditions, a judgment of the form, *it would be morally wrong of P to D*, has to be understood as elliptical for a judgment of the form, *in relation to moral framework M, it would be morally wrong of P to D*. Similarly for other moral judgments.

If the QA terminology makes sense and if claims using that terminology have "truth" conditions, then even a moral relativist can suppose that, when Veronica and Archie use QA terminology to disagree about raising animals for food, there is after all an answer to their dispute. What one says is true and what the other says is false. But the relativist will deny that there is an *objective* answer and so will deny that the true answer is *objectively* true, since according to the relativist the dispute can be resolved, if it is resolved, only by moral bargaining, not by objective inquiry, and there is no objectively privileged moral framework. If the QA terminology makes sense, the issue of moral relativism must be conceived as an issue about objectivity, not an issue about truth.

3.5 Is there a Need for Relative Moral Judgments?

Let us return to the issue between moral relativism and nihilism. Moral relativism denies that we should simply give up on morality in the way that a religious skeptic might give up on religion. There are practical reasons to want to retain morality and relative moral judgments.

Now quasi-absolutism claims to provide a nonrelativistic usage that may be more useful than a purely relativistic usage in allowing a way to express moral disagreements between people with different moral frameworks. If so, does that mean we can simply forget about relative moral judgments? No, because quasi-absolutist moral judgments are best seen as projections of relative moral judgments and are unintelligible apart from an understanding of such relative judgments.

4

Universality of Practical Reasons?

In one common view of morality (Nagel, 1970; Gewirth, 1977) morality contains requirements that apply to everyone. Furthermore, in this view, when a moral requirement applies to someone, that person has compelling reasons to do what he or she is required to do. But can we accept both of these propositions?

As we shall see, it is by no means obvious that everyone has compelling reasons to satisfy the moral requirements that you accept. I discuss that issue in the present chapter. If you have to agree that others may not have compelling reasons to satisfy your moral requirements, this raises a question: in what sense can you suppose that the moral requirements you accept apply to people who do not have compelling reasons to act in accordance with them? I will discuss that issue in chapter 5.

4.1 Compelling Reasons

Let me begin discussion of this issue with some terminological proposals, relating judgments about a person's reasons to judgments about what is reasonable for that person. We will be concerned quite generally with reasons for a person S to D, where D might specify a belief, an action, or anything else for which someone might have reasons. So, the following remarks are meant to apply to such instances as "reasons to believe that Fermat's Last Theorem has been proved," "reasons to eat less meat," and "reasons to be embarrassed by one's brother's behavior."

Let us say that a person S has *sufficient reasons* to D if and only if: given S's overall situation it would be (at least) reasonable for S to D. S might have reasons to D that are not sufficient reasons to D, if the reasons are undercut or outweighed by other considerations. Having sufficient reasons to D is compatible with also having sufficient reasons to do something else instead. Given a choice of apples or routes to the shore, any of several possibilities might be reasonable.

I will say that S has *compelling reasons* to D if and only if: all things considered, it would be reasonable for S to D and it would not be reasonable for S not to D.

I will suppose that to say "there are reasons" for S to D is to say roughly that there are considerations such that S would have reasons to D if S were aware of those considerations.[1] This is inexact, since it might be true that S could become aware of the reasons only in a way that would affect what reasons there are for S, but this complication does not affect what I will be saying, since I will considering only situations in which we are to assume S is aware of all relevant considerations.

So, to say that there are compelling reasons for S to D is to say there are considerations the awareness of which would provide S with compelling reasons to D. So, if there are compelling reasons for S to D but S does not D, then, either S is unaware of those reasons or S is being unreasonable.

Or, to put the matter in another and more useful way: if S does not D, S is aware of all relevant considerations, and S is not in any way unreasonable, then it is not the case that there are compelling reasons for S to D.

---

[1] There may or may not be a suggestion that the reasons that there are for S to D are relatively "available" to S. They might be facts that S ought to be able to infer from things S already knows, or facts he could become aware of by looking around or doing a relatively simple investigation, as opposed to theorems that are not within the competence of any living mathematician or facts known only to people on the other side of the world.

4.2 Failing to Have Compelling Moral Reasons

With respect to fairly fundamental requirements of morality, such as rules against stealing and killing, it seems easy to think of actual people who do not observe these rules who seem otherwise rational and well informed. Such people include successful criminals who lead enjoyable lives and are able successfully to escape punishment for violations of the principle that one should not kill other people. There are also politicians mainly interested in political power at any cost. There are people with odd moral views, who for example take cats to have supreme moral value. There are so-called sociopaths and simple egoists who are interested only in themselves.

It is easy to think of such people who lack motivation to observe basic moral requirements, and not because of any nonmoral ignorance on their part, any failure to reason correctly, any weakness of will, or any other sort of failure to appreciate reasons to observe the requirement in question. It is difficult to see how such people could nevertheless have compelling reasons to observe the moral requirements.

True, there are philosophical arguments purporting to show that there are reasons for such a person to observe one or another moral requirement, reasons that the person is allegedly failing to appreciate (Nagel, 1970; Gewirth, 1977; Darwall, 1983; etc.), but these arguments do not work. The people mentioned make no objective mistake in reasoning in rejecting these arguments. (I say more about this, below.)

Considerations of cases suggests that what moral requirements a person has compelling reasons to follow will depend on that person's principles and values. This conclusion is further confirmed by a natural account of reasons and reasoning: A person's reasons are determined by the reasoning that is available to the person or would be available if the person had more information or had certain obstacles to good reasoning removed. Furthermore, practical reasoning, like other reasoning, is a kind of change in view. What conclusions are supported by practical reasoning depends on where one starts, that is it depends on one's initial desires, goals, intentions, beliefs, and values. If people have different enough starting positions with respect to their desires, goals, intentions, and values, then they will be subject to different practical reasons even given the facts as they really are (Harman, 1986).

True, a different theory of practical reasoning like Gewirth's (1977) or Nagel's (1970) implies everyone has compelling reasons to observe certain basic moral requirements, so it is necessary to consider those theories to see whether one of them is more plausible than the alternative view which supposes that one's moral reasons depend on what moral framework one accepts. I will say more about these other theories below. But I must first clear up a loose end connected with the possibility of the quasi-absolutist use of moral terminology as discussed in the preceding chapter.

4.3 Two Kinds of Moral Reasons

The argument for the nonuniversal character of moral reasons notes that some people who are not motivated by rules against stealing or injury to others do not seem to be ignorant of relevant facts and do not seem to be in any way irrational or unreasonable.

Now the term *unreasonable* is a normative term and is sometimes used to express a moral judgment (Miller, 1992, pp. 352–9). There is a sense of the term in which those who believe in not harming others might call someone who does not care about others "unreasonable."

According to moral relativism, whether someone is reasonable or unreasonable in this sense is a relative matter, depending on the values in question. In relation to certain values *V* the egoist is being unreasonable. In relation to his own values, though, the egoist is being quite reasonable. And the relativist presumably does not want to suppose that the test of whether someone has a reason to do something is whether the agent's failure to do it would show the agent was unreasonable in relation to a set of values other than the agent's!

But now we must allow for quasi-absolutism. If the quasi-absolutism makes sense, the moral relativist can suppose that the test of whether someone has a reason to do something is whether the agent's failure to do it would show the agent to be UNREASONABLE (using all capital letters to indicate QA usage).

Under this construal, if our argument for moral relativism is correct, it is not an objective matter what reasons someone has. To make this explicit, we might speak of REASONS, as opposed to (objective) reasons.

Reasons are objective reasons; there is a matter of objective fact about them. REASONS are normative; there is not a matter of objective fact about them.

Now, when a moral relativist says that there are no moral demands that all rational agents have compelling reasons to follow, objective reasons are meant, reasons of the sort that carry weight with the agent, or would carry weight apart from objective defects in the agent, failure to follow or objectively appreciate some argument or other reasoning, and lack of objective information.

4.4 Morality as Entailed by Objective Facts

Let us say that P "entails" Q if and only if there are no possible situations in which P could be true and Q not true.[2] Suppose that P is objectively true and suppose that P entails Q in this sense. Does it follow that Q is also objectively true?

This does *not* follow, since the entailment may not hold objectively. A moral relativist might have the moral view that all possible cases of torturing a baby for fun are WRONG. The moral relativist does not take this to be an objective truth, but does accept it as a moral "truth." In other words, the moral relativist takes it to be true that torturing a baby for fun is

---

[2] This is similar to Thomson's definition (Thomson, 1990, p. 6), "I will throughout say that a statement Q is entailed by a statement P (and that P entails Q) if and only if, if P is true, then so must Q also be true." Other authors sometimes use the term "entails" differently.

always and necessarily WRONG. Suppose that P is the proposition that a certain act is an act of torturing a baby to death for fun and Q is the proposition that the act in question is WRONG. Then the moral relativist can suppose that Q is entailed by the objective truth P without the relativist's being committed to supposing that Q is objectively true, since the relativist does not suppose that the entailment holds objectively in this case.

4.5 Morality as a Commitment of Rational Agency

As mentioned above, philosophers occasionally argue that it can be objectively shown that there are certain basic moral principles to which all rational agents are committed. Kant, famously, argued in this way for his "categorical imperative," and similar claims have been vigorously defended by Gewirth (1977). But none of the many arguments that have been given for this claim are any good.

One argument of this sort has you consider your own situation from someone else's point of view, a point of view in which "positions are reversed," where this consideration is supposed to show you, after reflection, that you have a reason to take the other person's interests into account in the present unreversed situation. To suppose you do not have a compelling reason to take the other person's interests into account in this situation is to suppose the other person would not have compelling reason to take your interests into account in the reversed situation. It is argued that, since you cannot accept the other person's not taking your interests into account in the reversed situation, you would be inconsistent not to take the other person's interests into account in the actual situation.

This argument rests on an equivocation concerning what it is to "accept" a person's doing something, which may be either (a) to want the other person to do it (or at least not want the other person not to do it) or (b) to think the other person has compelling reasons to do it. The sense in which you cannot "accept" the other person's ignoring your interests is sense (a). You do not *want* the other person to ignore your interests. From *your* point of view it ought not to be the case that the other person ignores your interests. It does not follow that you cannot "accept" the other person's ignoring your interests in sense (b). You may very well realize that from the other person's point of view, it ought to be the case that the other person ignores your interests. You may see that the other person indeed has sufficient reasons to ignore your interests.

4.5.1 Gewirth's Argument

According to Gewirth, you are committed as a rational agent to thinking of your freedom and well being as "necessary goods." So, he argues, you are committed to supposing others must not interfere with your obtaining and possessing freedom and well being. And this, Gewirth claims, is to suppose you have a right to freedom and well being simply because you are a rational agent. But, he concludes, that supposition commits you to allowing that all other rational agents have the same right and, therefore, that you must not interfere with their obtaining and possessing freedom and well being.

This is a brief sketch of an argument that Gewirth spends many pages elaborating and defended. The argument has received extensive commentary, and Beyleveld (1991) has (with Gewirth's blessing) written a long book explaining the argument and replying to critical objections.[3] Nevertheless, we can be confident that the argument is invalid.

A key step in the argument goes like this. Assume:

(1) I am committed to taking a negative attitude toward interference with my own freedom and well being.

From that, Gewirth wishes to derive the following conclusion.

(2) I am committed to supposing that I have a right to my freedom and well being.

---

[3] On pages 273–6, Beyleveld explains that I have elsewhere misrepresented Gewirth's Argument (Harman, 1983, p. 17).

But, clearly, (2) does not follow objectively from (1),[4] since a moral nihilist (for example) can coherently accept (1) without supposing that there are such things as rights and without making any mistakes of nonnormative fact or objective reasoning.

4.6 Defective Agents

Some philosophers and psychologists have argued that anyone who fails to accept certain basic moral requirements can be shown to be objectively defective as an agent. For example, Nagel (1970) argues that to think you have no reasons to try to satisfy the interests of others is to be a "practical solipsist," because you deny the reality of others in your practical reasoning even if you accept their reality in your theoretical reasoning. And Kohlberg (1981) argues that there are stages of moral development leading to a sixth and highest stage at which people agree on basic moral principles. According to Kohlberg, people who do not yet accept these principles have an objectively defective, not fully developed conception of morality.

But neither Nagel nor Kohlberg makes his case.

4.6.1 Nagel's Rejection of Practical Solipsism

Nagel's argument is that as a rational person who is not a solipsist you must acknowledge that a judgment of yours in the first person, like *I am five feet nine inches tall*, has the same "content" as the corresponding judgment in the third person, *That person is five feet nine inches tall*, except for a difference in perspective. Nagel argues further that your judgment, *I have compelling reasons to D* has "motivational content"; such a judgment is associated with motivation to D. He concludes that you are committed to supposing that the corresponding third-

[4] Beyleveld's discussion of this step of the argument (1991, pp. 95–7) is logically incoherent.

person judgment, *He has compelling reasons to D*, has "motivational content" too. Otherwise, he claims, you would be a "practical solipsist," even if not a theoretical solipsist. But to be committed to taking third-person judgments of this sort to have motivational content is to be committed to being motivated to help others do things they have reasons to do or want, according to Nagel.

Nagel's argument depends crucially on what we might call an "objectivity principle," namely that first- and third person-judgments have the same "content," apart from considerations of perspective. Nagel argues for the objectivity principle by noting that it seems to hold for certain judgments and by observing that certain violations of the principle are associated with solipsism, namely cases in which you think your judgments about your own feelings have an entirely different content from your judgments about the feelings of others.

But this leaves obscure exactly what is to count as part of the "content" of a judgment for the purposes of the objectivity principle. Consider judgments about pains. First-person judgments about pains have what we might call "affective content," in that if you sincerely judge you are in pain, you normally are in pain. Does Nagel's objectivity principle have the consequence that your third-person judgments should have a similar affective content, so that you can only judge that another person is in pain if it hurts you too? That consequence would be absurd. So, it seems the objectivity principle cannot apply to "affective content." But then the objectivity principle is not perfectly general and some argument is needed to show it should be applied to what Nagel calls "motivational content." Since (so far as I know) Nagel has not offered any such argument, he has not shown there is anything (nonmorally) defective about the practical reasoning of an agent who fails to take the interests of others as providing him or her with reasons.

4.6.2 Kohlberg's Stages of Moral Development

Kohlberg's argument combines empirical and philosophical considerations. His theory says that there are six stages of moral development, two "pre-conventional" stages, two "conventional" stages, and two "post-conventional" stages. In the first stage, a child takes doing what is right to be a matter of obeying authority, avoiding punishment, and not harming others. In the second stage, doing what is right also includes making fair deals in terms of concrete exchange and satisfying immediate needs. The third and fourth stages are centered around socially approved virtue and character (third stage), or social rules and principles (fourth stage). At the end of the fourth stage people begin to think about the whole system of societal morality and its justification. Some people become and remain skeptical or relativistic at this point; others progress to the post-conventional fifth stage in which they take people to have rights that are prior to society. Finally, at the sixth stage people come to realize that there are universal ethical principles all humanity ought to follow, principles of respect for other persons as ends in themselves. Social rules are judged by considering whether one would find them acceptable if one did not know one's place in society.

Kohlberg hypothesizes that moral development from one stage to the next occurs as someone acquires a more adequate conception of morality. He suggests that stage six is the highest stage reached because it represents the most adequate conception of morality. However, his extensive evidence does not seem to support such a strong hypothesis. The key issue concerns what happens after Stage IV, because the development from Stage I (obedience to authority) to Stage IV (acceptance of the authority of the moral rules of your society) involves nothing more than coming to appreciate conventional morality. But Kohlberg's actual data do *not* indicate a *single* direction of development from Stage IV on. Development from that point occurs when people raise questions about the rules of their own society and become aware of alternative possibilities. Kohlberg's data (and common observation as well) show that at this point people in fact go off in *various* directions. Many people come to accept something like the egoism of the second stage (leading Kohlberg to speak of a "Stage $4\frac{1}{2}$"). Some people become moral relativists. Some become utilitarians, taking morality to be concerned with the promotion of the general happiness. Some decide moral rules are binding only on those who consent to them. Some try to reach their own arrangements with a "counter culture." And there are, as we all know, many other points that people sometimes take. Kohlberg's fifth stage is not a specially privileged option; indeed, it is not a single option at all but a collection of some of the possibilities, namely those Kohlberg was most in sympathy with: for example, it includes both utilitarianism and also the competing view that moral principles are binding only on those who consent to those principles. Kohlberg's sixth stage simply seems to represent the sort of thinking Kohlberg himself thought to be most adequate. I see nothing in Kohlberg's data that supports a privileged position for his fifth and sixth stages.

True, Kohlberg does offer an independent argument of sorts for the greater adequacy of his fifth and sixth stages. The argument was an argument from philosophical authority: certain philosophers favor a conception of morality that is more in accord with Stage V reasoning than with earlier stages and is even more in accord with Stage VI reasoning. But this is not very impressive since there are many philosophers (and others) who favor other conceptions of morality that are not particularly in accord with Kohlberg's stages V and VI.

Other objections have been raised to Kohlberg's approach and to similar approaches by Piaget and Gilligan. Piaget (1956) hypothesized general stages of cognitive development, including moral development; Kohlberg's (1981) and Gilligan's (1981) proposals are within the same framework. Although there has been considerable philosophical interest in these ideas (Rawls, 1971; Kittay and Meyers, 1987; Flanagan, 1991), Carey (1990) points out that the hypothesis of unified cognitive stages has not stood up well to experimental test.

Furthermore, Darley and Shultz (1990) observe that the principles followed when a child thinks about a situation morally may not be the same as the principles expressed when the child defends one or another judgment. The principles the child actually uses in its own reasoning may not be easily accessible to it. The approach pursued by Piaget, Kohlberg, and Gilligan looks at the principles used to rationalize or defend decisions. But when other investigators have studied the principles children actually follow, they find children using fairly sophisticated moral reasoning at relatively young ages.

Darley and Shultz also point out that since Kohlberg discusses fairly complex situations, his results may have little to do with children's moral reasoning and more to do with their ability to report on the reasoning they do.

So, we can safely reject Kohlberg's claims about practical reasons just as we can reject similar claims by Kant, Nagel, and Gewirth. Different people have different basic objective reasons to do things and there are people with no objective reasons to follow our basic principles of morality.

5
Judgments about Outsiders

5.1 Tolerance

In a very useful discussion, Wong (1984, chapter 12) observes that combining moral relativism with a widely-held moral view has implications for tolerance of other cultures. The moral view in question says "that one should not interfere with the ends of others unless one can justify the interference to be acceptable to them were they fully rational and informed of all relevant circumstances. To do otherwise is to fail to treat them with the respect due rational beings" (p. 181). Wong calls this the "justification principle."

Consider a moral vegetarian who accepts the justification principle, who also accepts moral relativism and agrees, in particular, that moral vegetarianism represents values that can be rejected without objective mistake of fact or reasoning. This would provide the moral vegetarian with at least some reason to try to tolerate nonvegetarians.

As Wong points out, exactly the same considerations apply to the case of abortion. Consider someone who rejects abortion as murder but also accepts moral relativism as well as the justification principle. This individual believes that the rejection of abortion does not represent the one objectively true morality but arises from values that some but not others accept. Such a person has a reason to be tolerant of those who are not opposed to abortion. It might very well come to seem inappropriate to have laws against abortion, given the large numbers of people who are not opposed to abortion, because these laws cannot be justified to the people they restrict.

Widespread acceptance of the justification principle might itself be explained by the hypothesis that overall social morality arises from conventional understandings reached among people of diverse backgrounds and personal ideals.

This is not to say that relativism leads to tolerance of everything. As Wong also points out, although the justification principle provides a reason not to interfere with actions of others, this reason has to be weighed against other considerations.

Moral relativists need not be tolerant of harms committed by criminals who have not accepted conventional morality. There are strong self-interested reasons for us to include in our moral understanding the proviso that we can use force against those who harm others. There are not similarly strong, self-interested reasons for vegetarians to include in their moral understanding the condition that they can use force against those who raise animals for food.

But, of course, self-interested reasons are not the only reasons that might play a role, here. Moral vegetarians may value animal life very highly, and that can lead them to favor laws against cruelty to animals, against animal experimentation, against certain methods of treating livestock, and so forth. But moral vegetarians must also as a practical matter reach some understanding with the rest of us; and that is where the pressure of tolerance comes from. On the other hand, in a society in which all but a very few people were moral vegetarians, there might be little or no reason for them to tolerate anyone's raising animals for food.

The question of tolerance of abortions is harder to judge. Much opposition to abortion might survive acceptance of moral conventionalism. If enough people were opposed to allowing abortions, those opposed might take it to be unnecessary to reach a compromise with those who favor allowing abortions. Anti-abortionists might continue to accept principles allowing the use of force to prevent abortions. But as a practical matter, it is hard to believe that this could prevail in anything like present circumstances in the United States because of the many people who perceive their own interests to lie on the other side. These other people will not in these circumstances agree to allowing force to be used to prevent abortions. Eventually some sort of compromise must be reached, one mostly favoring the pro-abortion side, since self-interest plays no direct role on the other side.

5.2 Objective Justifications and JUSTIFICATIONS

Recall Wong's justification principle, "that one should not interfere with the ends of others unless one can justify the interference to be acceptable to them were they fully rational and informed of all relevant circumstances." A complication arises because of the distinction between objective reasons and REASONS (see above, "Two Kinds of Moral Reasons" on pages 48–9). Presumably, we can also distinguish objective justifications and JUSTIFICATIONS. A JUSTIFICATION is an argument that it would be UNREASONABLE to reject. An objective justification is an argument that it would be objectively unreasonable to reject.

Then how should we understand Wong's justification principle? Does it require not interfering with someone unless we can present an objective justification or does it merely require presenting a JUSTIFICATION. An anti-abortionist who thinks it is WRONG not to respect the rights of foetuses might suppose it UNREASONABLE to reject appeal to those rights as an JUSTIFICATION of laws against abortion. So, allowing JUSTIFICATIONS would seem to make the principle empty. Since many people do seem to accept a substantive principle that tends toward tolerance in the presence of moral relativism, we can conclude that many people accept a justification principle that does require objective justification.

5.3 Judgments about Moral Reasons

Now we come to a further issue. A spectator can evaluate an agent who has different values from those of the spectator. The spectator may or may not have to take the agent's values into account, depending on the sort of moral judgment he makes of the agent. An interesting issue arises for moral judgments by moral relativists that attribute reasons to an agent. For example, the judgment, "Albert ought morally to help out with the picnic," might be used to say that Albert has compelling moral reasons to help out with the picnic. Other moral judgments do not attribute compelling reasons to the agents mentioned. For example, the judgment "it is terrible that the tiger attacked the children at the zoo," would not normally be used to say either that the tiger had compelling moral reasons to refrain from attacking the children or that the children had compelling moral reasons to refrain from being attacked. The judgment says that it was bad *that* the tiger attacked the children, not that it was bad *of* the tiger to have attacked the children, or bad *of* the children to have been attacked.[1]

People can make judgments about people that resemble this sort of judgment about the tiger. Suppose Mabel takes Hitler's actions to be a great evil and also believes that Hitler's values were sufficiently perverse that they provided Hitler with no reason to refrain from acting as he acted. Mabel may then view Hitler as in some ways similar to the tiger. Although she judges Hitler to be a great evil, she may find that she is no more able to judge that it was wrong *of* Hitler to have acted as he acted than to judge that it was wrong of the tiger to have attacked the children.

The analogy between the case of Hitler and the case of the tiger is not perfect. It may be more appropriate for Mabel to think of Hitler as an *enemy*. Still, she will judge that Hitler's actions are terrible in relation to her side even if these same actions are not terrible in relation to the other side with its Nazi outlook, just as Alice views rain as bad for her team even if it is good for Bertie's team. Mabel can think that we need to destroy Hitler, our enemy, while believing that Hitler may be justified in relation to his own framework.

I do not claim that Mabel's view of Hitler is required or even that it is very plausible, only that it is intelligible. It may very well be a false view of Hitler.

---

[1] I am indebted to Thomas Nagel for this example.

But suppose for the sake of argument that Hitler's moral outlook did not require him to respect all people and did not give him reasons to refrain from ordering the extermination of the Jews. Finally, suppose for the sake of argument that Hitler did not have a compelling reason from any source to refrain and, indeed, had a sufficient reason to proceed with his evil plans. Then any moral judgment that implied that Hitler did have a compelling reason to refrain could not be true. (If P is not true and Q implies P then Q is not true.) So, the claim that Hitler ought morally not to have ordered the extermination of the Jews would not be true, if in fact Hitler did not have compelling reason to refrain and if the claim that Hitler ought morally not to have ordered the extermination of the Jews implies that Hitler had compelling reasons to refrain.

The issue is complicated by the possible ambiguity between reasons in the evaluative sense and reasons in the objective sense, between REASONS and objective reasons. Recall that, roughly speaking, the test of whether P has compelling REASONS to D is that it would be UNREASONABLE for P not to D, whereas the test of whether P has compelling objective reasons to D is that it would be objectively unreasonable for P not to D.

Mabel might use the phrase *morally ought* to imply that an agent had compelling objective reasons or to imply that an agent only had compelling REASONS. If she uses *morally ought* in the second of these ways, she might be able to say after all that Hitler morally ought to have refrained, because she might hold that Hitler did have compelling REASONS to refrain even if she does not believe that Hitler had compelling objective reasons to refrain.[2] That is, Mabel might be able to suppose that Hitler was UNREASONABLE, even if she is not able to suppose that Hitler was not objectively unreasonable in acting as he did.

---

[2] In previous writings about moral reasons I have failed to appreciate this point.

5.4 Critic Relativity and Agent Relativity

We have now considered two different, if related, kinds of moral relativity. First, there is the claim that what is morally good, right, or just is always relative to a moral framework. Second, there is the claim that the objective moral reasons an agent has depend upon the agent's desires, goals, aims, intentions, and values and, in particular, that there is enough variation so that an agent may fail to have compelling objective reasons to act on principles that a given critic endorses.

Objective judgments of moral relativists who accept both claims will be subject to two sorts of linguistic relativity. First, consider objective moral judgments in which there is no explicit indication of the relevant moral framework. Ordinarily, these judgments will be made in relation to a framework that is presupposed to be shared between the critic and his audience. Such judgments illustrate *critic relativity*: there is a relativity to the critic's values.[3]

Second, consider moral judgments like, "*A* ought morally to *D*," or, "It would be wrong of *C* to *G*," taken as implying that an agent has compelling objective reasons to do something. Such judgments illustrate *agent relativity*: there is a relativity to the agent's values.

If critic and agent accept sufficiently different moral frameworks, the critic can only make certain sorts of judgments about the agent. The critic can express certain evaluations of the agent in relation to the critic's moral framework, like "Hitler was a great evil." And the critic can make reason implying judgments in relation to the agent's morality, "Hitler was doing the morally right thing for a Nazi to do." But the critic cannot make objective reason implying judgments in relation to his (the critic's) morality. The critic will not be able to say, for example, "It was morally wrong of Hitler to have acted in that way," if the critic is a moral relativist who supposes that Hitler did not have a compelling objective reason to refrain from acting as he did is

---

[3] Lyons (1976) calls this "appraiser relativism".

using *morally wrong* so as to imply that the agent had compelling objective reason to refrain.

As a moral relativist, in judging other people, should you judge them in the light of your values or in the light of their values? It depends on what you say about them. If you are simply evaluating them, your own values are relevant. If you imply something about their objective moral reasons, then their values are relevant too. If you do not accept the moral framework in relation to which you are speaking, then you should make explicit what that framework is.

5.5 Conclusion

Let me summarize briefly. I began by explaining what moral relativism is and why I find it plausible: Moral relativism is a plausible inference from the most plausible account of existing moral diversity.

I then discussed moral conventions and moral bargaining. I discussed how taking morality to have a source in actual bargains, reached among actual people who have different powers and resources, might explain aspects of contemporary moral view, such as the relative strength of the duty not to injure others as compared with the duty to help others. I also discussed why animals tend to get ranked lower than people in most moral views. I argued that acceptance of this account of our moral views need not undermine those views.

I noted that self-conscious moral relativists might adopt a special quasi-absolutist terminology in order to express their disagreements with each other, and I explained that judgments made using that terminology can be counted true or false, even if not objectively true or false.

Next I turned more specifically to the issue about moral reasons. I noted that it is possible to adopt a quasi-absolutist way of talking about moral reasons, and that relativism is a claim about objective moral reasons. I discussed and rejected a number of arguments that there are universally applicable objective moral reasons, including arguments by Kant, Gewirth, Nagel, and Kohlberg.

Finally, I discussed connections between moral relativism and tolerance. I agreed with David Wong that moral relativists will tend to be more tolerant of the moral views of others at least in certain respects. I discussed the complex question of what judgments a moral relativist can make about others, especially judgments that have implications about the objective reasons that other agents may have.

Part II
Moral Objectivity

Judith Jarvis Thomson

Introduction to Part II

Suppose someone says "Abortion is wrong" or "Capital punishment is unjust" or "People ought to give more to the needy than they currently do give" and so on. That is, suppose someone asserts a moral sentence. It may happen that we wonder whether what he or she said is true, and that we then try to find out, figure out, work out for ourselves whether it is. Let us call this activity Moral Assessment.

It is very plausible to think that engaging in Moral Assessment is pointless if no moral sentences are true. For what could be the point of trying to find out whether moral sentences are true if the answer to the question whether they are is always and everywhere No?

It is very plausible to think, more strongly, that engaging in Moral Assessment is pointless if it is not possible to *find out* about any moral sentence that it is true. For even if some moral sentences are true, what could be the point of trying to find out which they are if that is not possible? Let us give this stronger thesis a name:

> Moral Assessment Thesis: Moral Assessment is pointless unless it is possible to find out about some moral sentences that they are true.

I take the idea that morality is 'objective' to be, at heart, the idea that this condition *is* met. No doubt some moral sentences are not true, and a fortiori, it is not possible to find out about them that they are true. (I am quite sure that "Everybody ought to kick a cat every Wednesday" is not true.) Perhaps, moreover, there are true moral sentences whose truth it is for one or another reason impossible to find out. Let us take moral objectivity to require only that it is possible to find out about some moral sentences that they are true:

> Thesis of Moral Objectivity: It is possible to find out about some moral sentences that they are true.

The Moral Assessment Thesis tells us a condition that must be met if Moral Assessment is not to be pointless; the Thesis of Moral Objectivity tells us that the condition is met.

What I here call the Thesis of Moral Objectivity is an epistemological thesis, and I should say a word about why I think that *it* is at the heart of the idea that morality is objective. After all, some philosophers who say they believe that morality is objective have taken the heart of that idea to be a metaphysical thesis, or a battery of metaphysical and linguistic theses, from which the Thesis of Moral Objectivity follows, as a welcome byproduct of moral objectivity but not its essence. My own view, however, is that it is precisely the securing of that byproduct – that the Thesis of Moral Objectivity should itself turn out to be true – that constrains what they will regard as an acceptable metaphysic of morality and account of the nature of moral discourse; and this precisely because they think that Moral Assessment is not pointless, but would be if the Thesis of Moral Objectivity were not true.

There are in any case close links between the metaphysical and linguistic on the one hand, and the epistemological on the other hand; they will emerge as we go.

Should we accept the Thesis of Moral Objectivity? There are a variety of arguments to the effect that we should reject it, and instead accept what I will call

> Moral Scepticism: It is not possible to find out about any moral sentence that it is true.

We will look at the most interesting of them.

6

Epistemological Arguments for Moral Secpticism

6.1 What might be called the traditional epistemological argument for Moral Scepticism has three premises. The first says that the crack or split in the universe of discourse between moral sentences on the one hand and factual sentences on the other hand is very deep: that is,

> Premise (i):   Moral sentences are not entailed by factual sentences.[1]

---

[1] A famous passage in Hume's *Treatise* is commonly taken to express this point:

> In every system of morality, which I have hitherto met with, I have always remark'd, that the author proceeds for some time in the ordinary way of reasoning, and establishes the being of a God, or makes observations concerning human affairs; when of a sudden I am surpriz'd to find, that instead of the usual copulations of propositions, *is*, and *is not*, I meet with no proposition that is not connected with an *ought*, or an *ought not*. This change is imperceptible; but is, however, of the last consequence. For as this *ought*, or *ought not*, expresses some new relation or affirmation, 'tis necessary that it shou'd be observ'd and explain'd; and at the same time that a reason should be given, for what seems altogether inconceivable, how this new relation can be a deduction from others, which are entirely different from it. (Hume, 1739, p. 469)

The second says that moral sentences are 'epistemologically parasitic on' factual sentences: that is,

> Premise (ii): The only way we have of finding out that a moral sentence is true is by finding out that certain factual sentences are true, and drawing the moral sentence as conclusion from them.

The third is a quite general constraint on finding out: that is,

> Premise (iii): If we come to believe a sentence S by finding out that certain sentences SS are true, and drawing S as conclusion from them, then our coming to believe S is our finding out that S is true only if the SSs entail S.

It can be seen that Moral Scepticism follows from these premises straightway. Is it possible to find out that a given moral sentence MS is true? Premise (ii) says this can be done only by finding out that certain factual sentences FSS are true, and drawing MS as conclusion from them. Premise (iii) says that our doing this is our finding out that MS is true only if the FSSs entail MS. But premise (i) says they do not.

What to do? It needs to be noticed that this traditional argument for Moral Scepticism is only a special case of something quite general. Moral Scepticism is itself only one variety of what might be called local scepticism; other familiar varieties are scepticism about the physical world, scepticism about the past, scepticism about the future, scepticism about other minds, scepticism about causality, and so on and on. And the arguments for each of these varieties of local scepticism all have the same structure. (Global scepticism is the view that it is not possible for anyone to find out about any sentence at all that it is true. A local sceptic may, but need not be, a global sceptic as well as a local sceptic, but the route to global scepticism is different, and I will ignore it in what follows.)

Here is the structure. First draw your hearers' attention to the crack in the universe of discourse between an interesting kind of sentence, the Ks, and a contrasting kind, the Cs. The Ks may be moral sentences; for them, the Cs are factual sentences. The Ks may instead be sentences about the physical world; for them, the Cs are perceptual reports. The Ks may instead be sentences in the past tense; for them, the Cs are sentences in the present tense. And so on.

Then invite your hearers to accept the following Premise (i*): the crack in the universe of discourse between Ks and Cs is very deep, that is, no Ks are entailed by Cs. Then invite your hearers to accept the following Premise (ii*): Ks are epistemologically parasitic on Cs, that is, the only way we have of finding out that a K is true is by finding out that certain Cs are true, and drawing the K as conclusion from them. Last, invite your hearers to accept the constraint on finding out that is expressed in Premise (iii) above. Scepticim now follows for each K-and-C pair.

So the traditional argument for Moral Scepticism lends no more weight to Moral Scepticism than do structurally similar arguments for scepticism about the physical world, the past, the future, other minds, and so on. Or so it certainly seems.

There is something deep in us and our language that tempts us to go down this road. We do find ourselves struck by cracks in the universe of discourse, and they do strike us as too deep to be crossed by entailment. These are not successive episodes: we do not focus on cracks that we think can be so crossed. (No one is struck by the difference between sentences about Greeks and sentences about northern Greeks.) Again, it does strike us that the one kind of sentence is epistemologically parasitic on the other; and this too is not a later episode, for we do not focus on a crack unless it seems to us that we can only get to one side *from* the other. (No one is struck by the difference between sentences about Greeks and sentences about other people.) In the case of each of the familiar varieties of local scepticism it was a major contribution to philosophy to have invited us to notice that particular crack in the universe of discourse. Lastly, we are strongly tempted by that constraint on finding out: how could it be thought that you have found a thing out – have really found it out – if the premises from which you drew it as conclusion do not entail it?

One response – a relatively modern response – is to reject the presupposition of the argument: this response says it is just a mistake to think of the universe of discource as cracked in the way that this or that instance of the argument declares it to be: a mistake that issues from concentrating on extreme cases, and overlooking the existence of a continuum between them. On some views, more strongly, the entire universe of discourse is a seamless web.

Another, more traditional response is to deny premise (i*) for this or that K. Thus some moral philosophers have declared that moral sentences are equivalent to certain factual sentences (one who thinks Utilitarianism a necessary truth is one who makes this response), and if moral sentences are equivalent to factual sentences, then they are, a fortiori, entailed by them. Other philosophers have declared that sentences about the physical world are equivalent to perceptual reports (this view is called Phenomenalism), and here too, if there is equivalence, then there is, a fortiori, entailment. (It is of interest that, and a good question why, this move has been more popular for some Ks than for others – for example, more popular for moral sentences than for sentences about the physical world.)

Yet another traditional response is to deny premise (ii*) for this or that K. Thus some moral philosophers have declared that we have a direct insight into moral truths, and need not reach them from factual truths – they credit us with moral intuition, or a moral sense like but different from the more familiar senses.[2] (And here too it is of interest that, and a good question why, this move has been more popular for some Ks and not others. For example, I know of no philosopher who has declared that we have a direct insight into the physical world, and need not reach conclusions about it by way of perception.)

None of those responses has seemed entirely satisfying to most philosophers, however.

Some philosophers instead reject Premise (iii). Is it really right to think that we haven't found a thing out if the premises

---

[2] Other moral philosophers have declared that some moral sentence are self-evident necessary truths, and that we can find out their truth by direct inspection, and thus *neither* by finding out that factual sentences are true and drawing the moral sentence as conclusion from them, *nor* by the use of a specifically moral intuition. Still others have replied that no sentence can be both a moral sentence and a self-evident necessary truth.

from which we drew it as conclusion do not entail it? Sometimes, having found out that certain sentences SS are true, we draw a conclusion S from them where the SSs do not entail S, but their truth nevertheless lends weight to S, or constitutes evidence for S. If we came to believe S in that way, then of course the SSs from which we drew S as conclusion do not themselves guarantee that S is true. But why should it be thought that they have to in order for us to be marked as having found out that S is true? No doubt we haven't found out that S is true unless S *is* true. But the question here is why our grounds for believing S have *themselves* to guarantee that S is true in order for us to be marked as having found out that S is true. Why wouldn't it be good enough that our grounds for believing S are evidence for S, and S is true?

There is much more to be said about this response to Premise (iii); I am going to have to leave it open. What I suggest we do is to focus on one idea in it – consideration of that idea has suggested to some people that moral sentences are different. Indeed, consideration of it has been thought by some people to yield an argument for Moral Scepticism that has no structural analogue for any of the other varieties of local scepticism that we have taken note of.

6.2 The response to Premise (iii) that we looked at draws attention to the fact that we sometimes come to believe a sentence S by virtue of drawing it as conclusion from certain sentences SS which we have found out to be true, and which do not entail S but whose truth nevertheless is evidence for S. Suppose I find that it looks, feels, and sounds to me as if I am sitting in front of the fire. I conclude that I really am sitting in front of the fire. Why so? The sentence "It looks, feels, and sounds to me as if I am sitting in front of the fire" does not entail that I am; but its truth is surely evidence that I am.

Again, suppose we find that Smith has a bullet in his head, and Jones is standing over Smith's body with a smoking gun. We conclude that Jones killed Smith. Why so? The sentence "Smith has a bullet in his head, and Jones is standing over Smith's body with a smoking gun" does not entail that Jones killed Smith; but its truth is surely evidence that he did.

What does it come to for the truth of SS to be evidence for S? Surely this is the case only if the truth of S would connect in some close way with the truth of SS. An attractive recent account of the connection is this: the truth of SS is evidence for S just in case the truth of S would *explain* the truth of SS (see Harman 1965). The truth of "It looks, feels, and sounds to me as if I am sitting in front of the fire" is evidence for "I am sitting in front of the fire," and it seems plausible to think that it is so in that my really sitting in front of the fire would explain its looking, feeling, and sounding to me as if I am. Again, the truth of "Smith has a bullet in his head, and Jones is standing over Smith's body with a smoking gun" is evidence for "Jones killed Smith," and it seems plausible to think that it is so in that Jones's really having killed Smith would explain Smith's now having a bullet in his head and Jones's standing over his body with a smoking gun.

Can the truth of a factual sentence be evidence for a moral sentence? Well, are there any factual sentences whose truth would be explained by the truth of a moral sentence? Consider the moral sentence "Alice ought to give Bert a banana." Is there any factual sentence whose truth would be explained by the truth of that moral sentence? What difference to the world of facts would be made by its being or not being true that Alice ought to give Bert a banana? If Alice *thinks* she ought to give B a banana, then she may (or may not) give Bert a banana; what difference to what Alice thinks and therefore does, or to anything else that happens, would it make if it were (or weren't) really true that Alice ought to give Bert a banana?

A new argument for Moral Scepticism now emerges. (I adapt it from Harman 1977, chap. 1.) The first premise says:

Premise (i@):   There is no moral sentence whose truth would explain the truth of a factual sentence.

The second flows from the account of evidence that we just took note of:

Premise (ii@): The truth of a factual sentence is evidence for a moral sentence only if the truth of the moral sentence would explain the truth of the factual sentence.

From these two premises there follows that there is no factual sentence whose truth is evidence for any moral sentence. The third premise is a minor variant on the thesis of epistemological parasitism that served as Premise (ii) of the traditional argument for Moral Scepticism:

Premise (iii@): The only way we have of finding out that a moral sentence MS is true is by finding out that certain factual sentences FSS are true, where the truth of the FSSs is evidence for MS, and drawing MS as conclusion from them.

Moral Scepticism plainly follows, for if, as the first two premises tell us, there is no factual sentence whose truth is evidence for any moral sentence, then – given the third premise – there is no way at all in which we can find out that a moral sentence is true.

I will call this the no-explanation argument for Moral Scepticism.

It is plausible to think that this argument has no structural analogue for any of the other varieties of local scepticism that we have taken note of. Perhaps Premise (i@) is true; that is, perhaps there is no moral sentence whose truth would explain the truth of a factual sentence. There surely are sentences about the physical world whose truth would explain the truth of a perceptual report: its being the case that I really am sitting in front of the fire would explain its looking, feeling, and sounding to me as if I am. There surely are sentences about the past whose truth would explain the truth of a sentence about the present: Jones's really having killed Smith would explain Smith's now having a bullet in his head and Jones's standing over his body with a smoking gun. So accepting the no-explanation argument for Moral Scepticism does not place us at risk of scepticism elsewhere.

Should we accept the no-explanation argument for Moral Scepticism?

6.3 Premise (i@) of the argument has provoked a considerable amount of discussion in recent years.

Nobody, I think, has the odd idea that the truth of a moral sentence might *directly* explain the truth of a sentence reporting a purely physical phenomenon, such as a bell's ringing or a whistle's blowing. But a number of people believe that the truth of a moral sentence might, and indeed sometimes does, explain the truth of a sentence reporting a certain kind of fact about a human being – namely that the human being believes such and such, or does such and such, or has such and such an attitude – and that the truth of a moral sentence might thereby, by transitivity, explain the truth of a sentence reporting a purely physical phenomenon. Thus, for example, they believe that the truth of the moral sentence "Alice's giving Bert a banana was just" might explain the truth of the factual sentence "Charles believes that Alice's giving Bert a banana was just," and thereby, by transitivity, explain the truth of "Charles is ringing the church bell in praise of Alice," and thereby, by transitivity, explain the truth of "A bell is ringing." In short, people who believe that the truth of a moral sentence MS might, and indeed sometimes does, explain the truth of a factual sentence FS think that all such explanations must be explanations of, or proceed via explanations of, truths about human beings' beliefs, actions, and attitudes. In shorter still, though they believe morality makes a difference to the world of facts, they believe it does so by way of making a difference to the lives of human beings.

Still, they do believe that morality does make a difference to the lives of human beings, and if they are right in this belief, then Premise (i@) of the no-explanation argument is false.

The first and most impressive defender of this idea is Nicholas Sturgeon (see Sturgeon, 1985). He offered two kinds of case in which, he said, the truth of a moral sentence really would explain the truth of a factual sentence about a human being.

Here is a simple case of Sturgeon's first kind. Suppose the factual sentence "Charles believes that Alice's giving Bert a banana was just" is true. What explains its truth? Well, how did

Charles come to have that belief? Suppose that Charles had been observing Alice carefully, and had realized that her giving Bert a banana was her keeping her word on an occasion on which it cost her a lot to so and she could have got away with not doing so; and suppose that it was for that reason that he concluded that Alice's giving Bert a banana was just. Sturgeon would have us agree that in this case, the truth of the moral sentence "Alice's giving Bert a banana was just" would explain the truth of the factual sentence "Charles believes that Alice's giving Bert a banana was just." That is, if we were to suppose that the moral sentence was true, we would have in hand an explanation of the truth of the factual sentence.

Another way to express the point is this. The factual sentence "Charles believes that Alice's giving Bert a banana was just" is by hypothesis true. So there is such a fact as the fact that Charles believes that Alice's giving Bert a banana was just. Let us call this a nonmoral fact ("factual fact" being a barbarism). Is the moral sentence "Alice's giving Bert a banana was just" true? If it were true, there would be such a moral fact as the fact that Alice's giving Bert a banana was just. Sturgeon's proposal is this: we can say that that (putative) moral fact would – if it really were a fact – explain the nonmoral fact. If we let the arrow represent explanation, we can picture Sturgeon's proposal as follows:

Alice's giving Bert a ——————▶ Charles believes that Alice's
banana was just   giving Bert a banana was just
(putative moral fact)   (nonmoral fact)

If this picture is acceptable, then given the account of evidence set out above, we can take the existence of the nonmoral fact to be evidence that the putative moral fact really is a fact.

Friends of the no-explanation argument would reject this picture. They would reply that wherever it may seem at first sight as if a moral fact would explain a nonmoral fact, there is always some other nonmoral fact that does the explanatory work. In this particular case (they would say), what does the explanatory work is the very nonmoral fact I mentioned in describing the case, namely the fact that Alice's giving Bert a banana was her keeping her word on an occasion on which it cost her a lot to so and she could have got away with not doing so. If it was Charles' realizing this that issued in his believing that Alice's giving Bert a banana was just, then it was *this* that explains his belief. Thus they would tell us that the picture we should accept is instead:

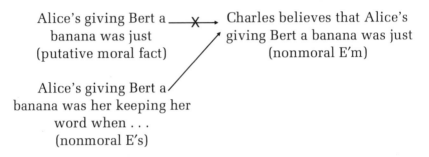

Alice's giving Bert a   **x**   Charles believes that Alice's
banana was just   giving Bert a banana was just
(putative moral fact)   (nonmoral E'm)

Alice's giving Bert a
banana was her keeping her
word when . . .
(nonmoral E's)

NO-MORAL-EXPLANATION PICTURE OF ALICE, BERT, AND CHARLES

Here "nonmoral E'm" means "nonmoral explanandum" (or "nonmoral fact to be explained"), and "nonmoral E's" means "nonmoral explanans" (or "nonmoral fact that does the explaining"); and the X indicates that, whether or not there is such a moral fact as the fact that Alice's giving Bert a banana was just, even if there were, it neither does nor would explain Charles's belief. Since, on this view, the putative moral fact does not explain the nonmoral E'm, the existence of the nonmoral E'm is not evidence that the putative moral fact really is a fact.

It is perhaps worth stress that the no-explanation argument is not an argument to the effect that there are no moral facts: it is an argument merely for the conclusion that we have no evidence that there are any. A friend of this argument might go on to conclude that there are no moral facts. ("If we have no evidence that there are any," he might say, "we might as well simplify our ontology and suppose there aren't.") But to go on to draw this conclusion is to be going on to draw a further conclusion *from* the conclusion of the no-explanation argument.

It is perhaps also worth stress that there is no room at all for the idea that the putative moral fact that Alice's giving Bert a banana was just is identical with nonmoral E's, and therefore does explain nonmoral E'm given that nonmoral E's explains nonmoral E'm. A fact F_1 is identical with a fact F_2 if and only if necessarily, the one exists if and only if the other exists; but it could have been the case that Alice's giving Bert a banana was just even though she had not given Bert her word that she would do so – there are other things that might have made her giving Bert a banana just, as, for example, that the banana she gave Bert belonged to him.

Sturgeon, interestingly enough, can and indeed might well accept the lower arrow in NO-MORAL-EXPLANATION PICTURE OF ALICE, BERT, AND CHARLES: that is, he might well agree that nonmoral E's explains nonmoral E'm. For he might say *both* that the putative moral fact explains Charles's belief *and* that the nonmoral E's explains Charles's belief. There is no incompatibility between these explanations: they are not in competition with each other. So we can depict Sturgeon's proposal as follows:

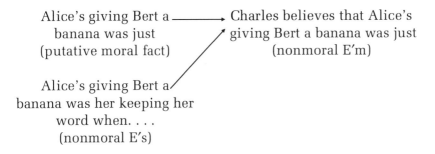

STURGEON PICTURE OF ALICE, BERT, AND CHARLES

The dispute between Sturgeon and the friends of the no-explanation argument is not over the acceptability of the lower arrow, it is rather over the acceptability of the upper one.

We can put the point in another way: the dispute between Sturgeon and his opponents is a dispute over whether if there is or were such a moral fact as that Alice acted justly, it is or would be *epiphenomenal* in this case.

The difficulty that faces us in deciding which party to this dispute we should agree with is that there is no agreed answer in the philosophical literature to the question how in general it is to be decided whether a given fact is epiphenomenal relative to a given explanandum.[3]

---

[3] The difficulty here arises even where it is not in doubt whether there are facts of the interesting kind. It is commonly said that social and political facts

Sturgeon's own ground for saying that the putative moral fact in the case of Alice, Bert, and Charles is non-epiphenomenal – is, as I will put the matter, *operative* – emerges as follows. Let us call the putative moral fact that Alice's giving Bert a banana was just MF. Then Sturgeon invites us to accept

> (1) If MF had not existed, nonmoral E's would not have existed.

Why should we accept (1)? Well, if Alice's giving Bert a banana hadn't been just, then her giving Bert a banana wouldn't have been her keeping her word when it cost her a lot to do so and she could have got away with not doing so – for an act that has that feature *is*, after all, a just act. Sturgeon then says we may suppose that in that case Charles would have realized that Alice's act was not her keeping her word when . . . – for by hypothesis Charles was observing her carefully – and that he would not then have believed that her act was just. So we are to accept not merely (1) but, more strongly,

> (2) If MF had not existed, nonmoral E's would not have existed, and therefore nonmoral E'm would not have existed.

From (2) we are on any view entitled to conclude

> (3) If MF had not existed, nonmoral E'm would not have existed.

---

supervene on facts about individuals, that psychological facts about individuals supervene on biological facts, and that biological facts supervene on physical facts – where facts of one kind X supervene on facts of another kind Y just in case *very roughly* what makes a fact of kind X exist is the existence of suitable facts of kind Y. (For more on the concept supervenience, see Kim (1993).) If facts of kind X supervene on facts of kind Y, then don't we have to conclude that facts of kind X are all epiphenomenal? For if it is facts of kind Y that make them exist, then don't we have to conclude that it is facts of kind Y that do whatever explanatory work is (thought to be) done by facts of kind X? This conclusion is unsatisfying, however, for it is very implausible to think that no social, psychological, or biological facts ever explain anything. One move that is sometimes made is to appeal to the very test for non-epiphenomenality that Sturgeon appeals to – but I will argue in the text below that that test is not adequate. (The concept superveni- ence will reappear in later footnotes in this chapter, and very briefly in chapter 8.)

Sturgeon's test for operativeness then tells us that from (3) we may conclude

(4) MF explains nonmoral E'm.

It is by appeal to the same counterfactual test for operativeness that Sturgeon argues that the putative moral fact is explanatory in all of his cases: we are to agree about each case that the case is one in which, if the putative moral fact MF had not existed, the nonmoral explanandum E'm would not have existed either, and we are to conclude from that that MF explains E'm.

But this counterfactual test for operativeness really won't do. Consider the following case. Donald was listening to a speech, and getting increasingly bored. He suddenly shouted "Boo!" at the speaker. In consequence, there was a loud "Boo!" sound on the tape recording of the speech. Now if there are any moral facts at all, there is such a moral fact as that Donald's shouting "Boo!" was rude. But that fact was surely epiphenomenal relative to the explanandum consisting in the presence of a "Boo!" sound on the tape: the fact of Donald's shouting's having been rude surely plays no role at all in explaining the fact of the "Boo!" sound on the tape – the case seems to me a positive paradigm of epiphenomenality, and we must therefore depict it as follows:

Donald's shouting "Boo!" —X→ There was a "Boo!" sound on the
        was rude   ↑   tape recording of the speech
   (putative moral fact)   /   (nonmoral E'm)
                          /
Donald's shouting "Boo!" was his
   shouting "Boo!" at the speaker
         in mid-speech
        (nonmoral E's)

PARADIGM EPIPHENOMENALITY[4]

[4] Countercases to the counterfactual test for operativeness are not restricted to morality: taking the case of Donald as model, it is easy enough to construct others. Passing that test is therefore not sufficient to mark a supervenient fact as operative.

On the other hand, this case passes the counterfactual test for operativeness if (and if so, in just the same way as) the case of Alice, Bert, and Charles does. For we may suppose that if Donald's shouting "Boo!" hadn't been rude, then it wouldn't have been the case that his shouting "Boo!" was his shouting "Boo!" at the speaker in mid-speech – shouting "Boo!" when you're all alone is one thing, shouting "Boo!" at a speaker in mid-speech is quite another, and very rude. So if we call the putative moral fact that Donald acted rudely MF, we can say

(1) If MF had not existed, nonmoral E's would not have existed.

Moreover, we can suppose that in that case there would have been no shout at all during the speech (no one else is as rude as Donald), and that there would therefore have been no "Boo!" sound on the tape. Thus we can say not merely (1), but, more strongly,

(2) If MF had not existed, nonmoral E's would not have existed, and therefore nonmoral E'm would not have existed.

From (2) we are on any view entitled to conclude

(3) If MF had not existed, nonmoral E'm would not have existed.

And Sturgeon's test for operativeness tells us that from (3) we may conclude

(4) MF explains nonmoral E'm.

In sum, then, Sturgeon's ground for saying that the putative moral fact in the case of Alice, Bert, and Charles is operative does not warrant that conclusion, for passing the counterfactual test for operativeness is not sufficient for operativeness.

How, then, is the dispute between Sturgeon and the friends of the no-explanation argument to be settled? I see no clean way of settling it: for the most part, we have to go case by case, and ask about each whether the relation between the putative moral fact and the nonmoral explanandum is or is not intuitively like the relation between them in the case of Donald.

I said "for the most part" because in some cases there is what I think a quite clean ground for thinking that the putative moral fact really is epiphenomenal. The case of Alice, Bert, and Charles is in fact one of them. Let us have another look at it.

6.4 Sturgeon would have us agree that the fact that Alice's giving Bert a banana was just would explain Charles's believing that it was. Thus we are to agree that a certain moral fact would explain a person's believing that there is such a fact. Under what conditions would *any* fact F explain a person's believing that there is such a fact as F? Suppose that Jones believes that a certain apple is red. We ask what explains his believing that the apple is red, and we are told: the apple is red. (We might well feel annoyed if we were offered only that by way of answer.) If an apple's being red is to explain a person's believing it is, there has to be some *way* in which it does. And what might that be?

One possibility is this: the apple's being red explains the existence of some mediating fact X such that Jones believes the apple is red because he takes X to be reason for believing the apple is red. So, for example, the apple's being red might explain the mediating fact X that the apple looks red to Jones, and Jones believes the apple is red because he takes X to be reason for believing the apple is red. Or the apple's being red might explain the mediating fact X′ that the apple looked red to Smith, which itself explains the further mediating fact X″ that Smith told Jones that the apple is red, and Jones believes the apple is red because he takes X″ to be reason for believing the apple is red. In these cases the apple's being red explains Jones's believing that the apple is red by transitivity.

There may be other possibilities as well, but this one is enough for present purposes. Suppose Jones believes an apple is red because he takes some fact X to be reason for believing the apple is red. Then it seems right to think that the apple's being red does explain Jones's believing it is red only if the apple's being red explains X.

A general thesis suggests itself: if a person believes that there is such a fact as F because he takes the fact X to be reason for believing that there is such a fact as F, then F explains the person's belief only if F explains X.

Let us now remind ourselves of the details of the case of Alice, Bert, and Charles. Alice's giving Bert a banana was her keeping her word when it cost her a lot to so and she could have got away with not doing so. By hypothesis, Charles observed what went on and therefore concluded that Alice's giving Bert a banana was just. So Charles believes that Alice's act was just because he takes a certain fact X – that Alice's act was her keeping her word when ... – to be reason for believing that Alice's act was just.

So if the general thesis I just set out is correct, then the fact that Alice's act was just would explain Charles's believing it was just only if the fact that Alice's act was just would explain X, the fact that Alice's act was her keeping her word when ... But the fact that Alice's act was just could not be thought to explain the fact that Alice's act was her keeping her word when ... Quite to the contrary: it is rather the fact that Alice's act was her keeping her word when ... that would explain the fact that Alice's act was just.

In short, in STURGEON PICTURE OF ALICE, BERT, AND CHARLES, explanation goes, not downwards from the putative fact MF to nonmoral E's, but rather upwards from nonmoral E's to the putative fact MF.[5]

This means that if we accept the general thesis, we must agree that the case of Alice, Bert, and Charles is not one in which a moral fact explains a nonmoral fact, and STURGEON PICTURE OF ALICE, BERT, AND CHARLES must be rejected. And hadn't we better accept the general thesis?

There is a general conclusion in the offing here. We very often believe that there is a moral fact MF because we have observed, or learned of, a nonmoral fact NMF that would explain there

---

[5] Philosophers who think there are moral facts think that they supervene on nonmoral facts (see footnote 3 above). In particular, they would say that the fact that Alice's act was just supervenes on the base fact that her act was her keeping her word when ... But explanation plainly goes, not from supervenient fact to base fact, but rather from base fact to supervenient fact.

being such a fact as MF. Given the general thesis, *no* such case is a case in which the moral fact MF would explain our believing that there is such a fact as MF.

6.5. Perhaps there are cases in which we believe that there is such a moral fact as MF because we have observed, or learned of, a nonmoral fact NMF that MF would explain (rather than being explained by)? Sturgeon's second kind of case might be thought to supply some.

In Sturgeon's second kind of case he appeals to a person's character to explain the person's having done what he did. Hitler instigated and oversaw the killing of millions of innocent people; that is a nonmoral fact. What explains it? The moral fact that Hitler was depraved, says Sturgeon.

Again, let us suppose that Alice had given her word that she would give Bert a banana, and that she did so, despite that fact that it was costly for her to do so and she could have got away with not doing so. What explains the nonmoral fact that consists in her giving Bert a banana? The moral fact that she is just, Sturgeon would say we can say. Thus he would invite us to accept the following picture:

Alice is just ———————→ Alice gave Bert a banana
(putative moral fact MF)   (nonmoral fact NMF)

STURGEON PICTURE OF ALICE

If we now add that Charles observed nonmoral fact NMF, and concluded from it that Alice is just, we can expand the picture as follows:

Alice is just⟶ Alice gave Bert a banana ⟶ Charles believes
(putative moral   (nonmoral fact NMF)   that Alice is just
  fact MF)

Here we (putatively) have a case in which a person, Charles, believes that there is such a moral fact as MF because he has observed a nonmoral fact NMF which MF would explain (rather than being explained by).

The expanded picture is acceptable only if STURGEON PICTURE OF ALICE is acceptable, so let us focus on that one.

But I think it need not detain us for very long, since, for the purposes of a person who wishes to rebut the no-explanation argument for Moral Scepticism, there is less in this case – indeed, there is less in all of the cases of Sturgeon's second kind – than meets the eye.

For let us ask: *how* would Alice's being just explain her giving Bert a banana? In what way, exactly? A person's being just is his or her being disposed to, or prone to, acting justly. And a person's being just might therefore explain his or her performing a particular just act. But a person's being just would explain his or her doing such and such – as it might be, giving Bert a banana – only on the assumption that his or her doing the such and such was just. But what entitles us to assume that Alice's giving Bert a banana was just?[6] On the account of evidence that we are working with, our having evidence for the (putative) moral fact that Alice's giving Bert a banana was just requires our having in hand some nonmoral fact that the moral fact would explain. In short, it requires our having in hand a nonmoral explanandum to fit into the following picture:

Alice's giving Bert a ⎯⎯⎯⎯⎯⎯⎯⎯→ ????
    banana was just   (nonmoral E′m)
   (putative moral fact)

In the preeding two sections, we looked at a candidate nonmoral explanandum, namely Charles's believing that Alice's giving Bert a banana was just; we need a new and better candidate if we are to take the proposal we are considering here seriously.

Perhaps an analogy would be helpful. Suppose it is said that religious facts would explain some non-religious facts, and therefore that some non-religious facts are evidence for religious facts. And suppose we are offered the following example: the religious fact that Alfred is Godly – that is, he is prone to

---

[6] Compare: Hitler's being depraved explains his instigating and overseeing the killing of millions of innocent people, only on the assumption that his doing that was evil. What entitles us to assume that it was?

acting in the ways God commands us to act in – explains the non-religious fact that Alfred eats fish on Friday. Alfred's being prone to acting in the ways God commands us to act in explains his eating fish on Friday only on the assumption that God commands us to eat fish on Friday; and what entitles us to make that assumption? What non-religious fact is *that* religious fact supposed to explain?

6.6. In section 6.3, I said I think that nobody has the odd idea that the truth of a moral sentence would directly explain the truth of a sentence reporting a purely physical phenomenon, such as a bell's ringing or a whistle's blowing. But (I said) a number of people believe that the truth of a moral sentence would explain the truth of a sentence reporting a certain kind of fact about a human being – namely that the human being believes such and such, or does such and such, or has such and such an attitude. Alternatively put, a number of people believe that a moral fact would explain the existence of this or that nonmoral fact – nonmoral facts consisting in a person's having a certain belief, or doing such and such, or having such and such an attitude. In short, they believe morality makes a difference to the world of facts, though only by way of making a difference to the lives of human beings.

We looked in sections 6.3 and 6.4 at a case in which it might be thought that a moral fact would explain a person's having a moral belief, in particular, Charles's believing that Alice's giving Bert a banana was just. In section 6.5, we looked at a case in which it might be thought that a moral fact would explain a person's doing something, in particular, Alice's giving Bert a banana. Are there cases in which it might be thought that a moral fact would explain a person's having a certain attitude? Sturgeon does not discuss any such case in detail, but he does give a hint. He says: "We point to injustice, along with poverty, as a cause of revolution, or of pressure for reform . . . " (Sturgeon 1986, p. 75) There are two ways of constructing cases from this hint. One way of taking the hint is to suppose that a society's being unjust might cause a revolution by causing members of the society to believe the society unjust and thereby causing them to rebel. Such a case would presuppose a possibility we have already met, namely that a moral fact might explain a person's having a moral belief. A second way of taking the hint is to suppose that a society's being unjust might cause a revolution by causing members of the society to have certain attitudes, their having of which then issues in their rebelling, perhaps by way of a moral belief, perhaps directly. The idea that a moral fact might explain a person's having a certain attitude is an idea we have not yet looked at.

How might such a case go? Here is a case described by Peter Railton. Many members of a certain society, which I will call Badland, are discontented – alienated, depressed, resentful of assertions of authority, and so on. Why so? Well, Badland discounts the interests of certain groups within it. Which groups? The poor, let us suppose. Railton would have us suppose that Badlandian discontent would be explained by Badland's injustice. Indeed, that the discontent is produced directly by the injustice: that is, we are not to suppose that Badland's injustice explains Badlandians' believing Badland unjust, and that *that* explains their discontent, we are rather to suppose that Badland's injustice (directly) explains their discontent.[7] So Railton would say we can depict this case as follows:

Badland is unjust ⟶ Many Badlandians are
(putative moral fact)   discontented
                          (nonmoral E'm)

Friends of the no-explanation argument would of course reject this picture. What would they say explains the nonmoral E'm here? The very nonmoral fact we were told about, namely that Badland discounts the interests of the poor. On their view, then, we must depict the case as follows:

---

[7] Railton says:

> discontent may arise because a society departs from social rationality ... [If] the interests of certain groups are being discounted, there will be potential for unrest that may manifest itself in various ways – in alienation, loss of morale, decline in the effectiveness of authority, and so on ... (Railton, 1986, p. 192).

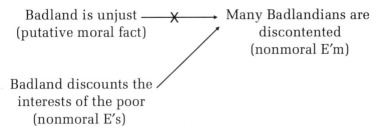

NO-MORAL-EXPLANATION PICTURE OF BADLAND

It is worth noticing that Railton can and indeed might well accept the lower arrow in NO-MORAL-EXPLANATION PICTURE OF BADLAND: that is, he might well agree that the nonmoral E's explains the nonmoral E'm. For he might say *both* that the putative moral fact explains the discontent *and* that the nonmoral E's explains the discontent. There is no incompatibility between these explanations: they are not in competition with each other. So we can depict Railton's proposal as follows:

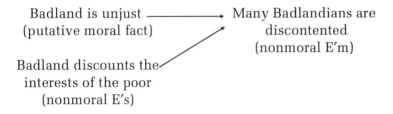

RAILTON PICTURE OF BADLAND

(Compare STURGEON PICTURE OF ALICE, BERT, AND CHARLES in section 6.3 above.)

Is Railton entitled to his upper arrow? How is the dispute between Railton and friends of the no-explanation argument to be settled? I said that I see no clean way of settling such disputes. We have to go case by case, and ask about each whether the relation

---

Moreover, Railton says that discontent may arise in the society even at a time at which the members believe their society to be just: he says that discontent may arise "well before any changes in belief about the society's justness occur . . ." So we are to suppose the discontent is not produced by way of a belief that the society is unjust, but rather directly by the society's injustice.

between the putative moral fact and the nonmoral explanandum is or is not intuitively like the relation between them in the case of Donald, which I depicted as follows:

Donald's shouting "Boo!" ──✗──▸ There was a "Boo!" sound on the
was rude ▸ tape recording of the speech
(putative moral fact) ╱ (nonmoral E'm)

Donald's shouting "Boo!" was his
shouting "Boo!" at the speaker
in mid-speech
(nonmoral E's)

PARADIGM EPIPHENOMENALITY

Now my own impression is that the case of Badland *is* intuitively like the case of Donald. I said that the fact of Donald's shouting's having been rude surely plays no role at all in explaining the fact of the "Boo!" sound on the tape; so similarly, it seems to me that the fact of Badland's being unjust plays no role at all in explaining Badlandian discontent – that Badland discounts interests by itself suffices.

At a minimum, it seems to me that the acceptability of RAILTON PICTURE OF BADLAND is not obvious: Badland is not a case in which a moral fact plainly explains a nonmoral fact. If a defense against Moral Scepticism has to rest on Badland's being such a case, then the defense seems to me to be very weak.

6.7 To summarize, we have looked at three cases that might be thought to refute

Premise (i@): There is no moral sentence whose truth would explain the truth of a factual sentence

of the no-explanation argument for Moral Scepticism. The first case (see sections 6.3 and 6.4) purports to be one in which a moral fact would explain a nonmoral explanandum consisting in someone's having a moral belief. The second (see section 6.5) purports to be one in which a moral fact would explain a nonmoral explanandum consisting in someone's doing something. The third (see section 6.6) purports to be one in which a moral fact would explain a nonmoral explanandum consisting in someone's having a certain attitude. And I have suggested that none of these cases succeeds – or anyway, none plainly succeeds – in being what it purports to be.

I have not of course shown, or even tried to show, that there cannot be a case in which a moral fact would explain a nonmoral fact consisting in a person's believing or doing this or that, or in a person's having such and such an attitude. (How *could* that be shown?) But it is hard to see how anyone could argue more successfully that there are such cases than Sturgeon and Railton did.

But if moral facts do not explain such nonmoral facts as that a person believes or does this or that, or as that a person has such and such an attitude, then they do not explain any nonmoral facts at all.

6.8 Is it a disaster for friends of Moral Objectivity to have to accept Premise (i@) of the no-explanation argument?[8] Not if they needn't accept

> Premise (ii@):   The truth of a factual sentence is evidence
> for a moral sentence only if the truth of the
> moral sentence would explain the truth of
> the factual sentence.

Should we accept Premise (ii@)?

What does it come to for the truth of SS to be evidence for S? I said: surely this is the case only if the truth of S would connect in some close way with the truth of SS. And I said that an attractive recent account of the connection is this: the truth of

---

[8] Sturgeon thinks that having to accept Premise (i@) would be a disaster for those who believe there are moral facts supervening on nonmoral facts. He says:

> even J. L. Mackie would have found it difficult to construct a view of moral properties which made them into stranger entities than does [Premise (i@)]. There they sit, fixed by the nonmoral properties of things; but they do nothing. (Sturgeon 1986, p. 75)

What he adverts to here is Mackie's view that moral properties would be too "queer" to count as respectable parts of a respectable ontology. See Mackie (1977).

SS is evidence for S just in case the truth of S would *explain* the truth of SS. I think that those ideas really did seem plausible. So Premise (ii@) seemed plausible.

But are those ideas right? Here again is one of the examples I gave in illustrating the ideas: I said that the truth of

> (1) Smith has a bullet in his head, and Jones is standing over Smith's body with a smoking gun

is evidence for

> (2) Jones killed Smith,

and it seems plausible to think that the truth of (1) *is* evidence for (2) in that the truth of (2) would explain the truth of (1).

But now consider another example. Surely the truth of

> (3) Dickenson is eating his way through a dozen hamburgers

is evidence for

> (4) Dickenson will soon feel ill.

Is it at all plausible to think that the truth of (3) is evidence for (4) in that the truth of (4) would explain the truth of (3)? Hardly. The fact (supposing it a fact) that Dickenson will soon feel ill would not explain the fact that he is eating all those hamburgers – quite to the contrary, it would be the fact that Dickenson is eating all those hamburgers that explained the fact (supposing it a fact) that he will soon feel ill.[9]

Arguably, if a sentence is in the past tense, as (2), is, then a fact about the present is evidence for it only if the truth of the past tense sentence would explain the existence of the fact about the present. But that cannot be said of sentences in the

---

[9] Warren Quinn makes the same objection to what I think is a first cousin of Premise (ii@). He says: "The presence of a cause might support an inference to its usual effect, but the effect would not explain the cause." See Quinn (1986), p. 541.

future tense, as (4) is. Presumably explanation goes in the other direction in the case of sentences in the future tense. That is, it is no less arguable that if a sentence is in the future tense, as (4) is, then a fact about the present is evidence for it only if the truth of the future tense sentence would *be explained by* the existence of the fact about the present.

We need not accept the general principles just drawn attention to. For our purposes, it is enough that the truth of SS can be evidence for S even though the truth of S would not explain the truth of SS, but instead the truth of S would be explained by the truth of SS.

And then why shouldn't we think that explanation can also go in that direction in the case of moral sentences? Why shouldn't we think that the truth of a nonmoral sentence might be evidence for a moral sentence where the truth of the moral sentence would *be explained by* the existence of the nonmoral fact?

And finding a moral sentence whose truth would be explained by the existence of some nonmoral fact looks to be easy enough. Here is an example. Suppose that Alice's giving Bert a banana was her keeping her word when it cost her a lot to do so and she could have got away with not doing so. That, it seems plausible to think, would explain the truth of "Alice's giving Bert a banana was just." No doubt the moral fact would be explained by this nonmoral fact in a way different from that in which the future fact reported by (4) would be explained by the fact about the present reported by (3): the latter explanation would be causal, the former would not. But not all explanation is causal – nor need it be. Compare a nonmoral example. Suppose that a painting P has the features such that art critics describe a painting with those features as impressionist.[10] The fact that P is an impressionist painting would be explained by its having those features, though not of course causally explained by its having them. It is certainly not required for P's

---

[10] The example here comes from Platts (1980). Platts says that a painting's being an impressionist painting supervenes on its having such features as I mention in the text; and as I said in footnote 5, explanation goes, not from supervenient fact to base fact, but rather from base fact to supervenient fact. So similarly would explanation go from nonmoral fact to moral fact if moral facts supervene on nonmoral facts.

having those features to be evidence that P is an impressionist painting that P's having those features causally explain P's being an impressionist painting. No more is it required for the fact that Alice's giving Bert a banana was her keeping her word when . . . to be evidence that her giving Bert a banana was just that her act's having had that feature causally explain her act's having been just.

It is arguable, however, that moral sentences differ in important ways from sentences to the effect that this or that painting is an impressionist painting, and that those differences make a difference. We should look at them.

7

Emotivism

7.1. There is a thesis, commonly called Emotivism, according to which the prospects for moral objectivity are even more dismal than was suggested by the arguments we looked at in the preceding chapter.

Emotivism is, more precisely, a cluster of interconnected theses.[1] There is first a semantic thesis, which emerges as follows. Consider the sentence "Alice is taller than Bert." That sentence has a truth-value; that is, either it is true or it is false. But not all sentences have truth-values. Consider "Go to the store!"; that sentence is neither true nor false. What about "Alice ought to give Bert a banana"? An Emotivist says that this sentence is like "Go to the store!" in having no truth-value. The Emotivist says the same of all moral sentences, and the first of the theses in the Emotivist cluster is therefore this:

    (I) No-Truth-Value Thesis: Moral sentences have no truth-values.

It is plain that if the No-Truth-Value Thesis is correct, so also is Moral Scepticism, for if no moral sentences have truth-values, then none are true, and a fortiori it is not possible to find

---

[1] I know of no Emotivist who has set the views out in exactly the way I describe in this section; however the views themselves – with differences that we need not stop over – may be found in a number of places. See Ayer (1946), Stevenson (1945), Hare (1952), Blackburn (1984), and Gibbard (1990).

out about any that they are true. But if Moral Scepticism is true because the No-Truth-Value Thesis is true, then our inability to find out about any moral sentence that it is true does not issue merely from constraints on what counts as finding something out, or from constraints on what counts as evidence for what, or from the epistemological parasitism of the moral on the nonmoral, or from any other epistemological difficulty which closer study might enable us to eliminate. Our inability issues rather from there being nothing moral to *be* found out. Our inability to find out that a moral sentence is true is like our inability to find out how much the round squares in the attic weigh: just as there are no round squares in the attic to be found out about, so also are there no moral truths to be found out about.

Again, if the No-Truth-Value Thesis is correct, it is no wonder that the crack in the universe of discourse between factual sentences and moral sentences is too deep to be crossed by entailment: nothing could entail what lacks a truth-value. Indeed, the crack is too deep even to be crossed by evidence: nothing could be evidence for what lacks a truth-value.

Why do people think the No-Truth-Value Thesis plausible? Let us first set out the remaining parts of the Emotivist cluster – the theses in it hang together.

If moral sentences have no truth-values, then none are true, so of course we must accept the following metaphysical thesis:

(II) No-Fact Thesis: There are no moral facts.

No wonder no moral facts would explain nonmoral facts: there are no moral facts to do any explaining.

If moral sentences have no truth-values, then what on earth are we doing in asserting them? A third, pragmatic, thesis says:

(III) Speech-Act Thesis: One who asserts a moral sentence merely displays an attitude, pro or con.

Thus if you assert "Alice ought to give Bert a banana," you are merely displaying a favorable attitude toward Alice's giving Bert a banana; if you assert "Alice ought not give Bert a banana," you are merely displaying an unfavorable attitude toward Alice's giving Bert a banana. It should be stressed: on this view, you are not, in asserting these sentences, *asserting that* you have the attitudes. What you are doing is merely *displaying* the attitudes, as you would if you said "Hooray to Alice's giving Bert a banana!" or "Boo to Alice's giving Bert a banana!"

If that is all we are doing in asserting moral sentences, then what is going on in a person who has a moral belief? Another metaphysical thesis gives the following answer:

(IV) No-Moral-Belief Thesis: There is no such thing as having a moral belief – being in the state that we (mistakenly) call "having a moral belief" is merely having an attitude, pro or con.

Thus you don't *believe* that Alice ought to give Bert a banana: you merely have a favorable attitude toward Alice's doing so. (No wonder, then, that in asserting "Alice ought to give Bert a banana" you are merely displaying a pro-attitude.) Similarly, you don't *believe* that Alice ought not give Bert a banana: you merely have an unfavorable attitude toward Alice's doing so. (No wonder, then, that in asserting "Alice ought not give Bert a banana" you are merely displaying a con-attitude.)

And now: why do people accept Emotivism? Some people have argued for Emotivism *from* Moral Scepticism.[2] (They, of course, would be arguing in a circle if they went on to argue *for* Moral Scepticism from Emotivism.) Others, however, have been moved by a more interesting argument for Emotivism, one that does not pass through Moral Scepticism. The argument I have in mind comes down to us from Hume.[3]

---

[2] See, for example, Ayer (1946), ch. 6. Ayer gets from Moral Scepticism to the No-Truth-Value Thesis (I) by way of the Principle of Verification.

[3] I interpret Hume as an Emotivist. It should be noted, however, that there are other interpretations of Hume's views, and the argument I will be laying out may not in fact really be what he had in mind. For present purposes, what matters is only the argument, whether or not it is Hume's.

All quotations from Hume are from Hume (1739). The passage I quote to state the first premise of the argument comes from Book III, Part I, section 1; Hume's argument for it is largely in Book II, Part III, section 3. Hume's statement of, and argument for, the second premise is in Book III, Part I, section 1.

7.2. The argument has two premises, of which the first is: "reason is perfectly inert." That is, there is no belief such that a person who has it is, by virtue merely of having it, favorably or unfavorably disposed toward something. Consider acquiring a belief. Hume says that our learning that if we do alpha, a state of affairs beta will exist, cannot make us be favorably disposed toward doing alpha unless we are already favorably disposed toward beta's existing. More generally, our learning that something (whether an act or anything else) has feature F cannot make us be favorably disposed toward the thing unless we are already favorably disposed toward F-ishness. But if *acquiring* a belief cannot by itself make us be favorably disposed toward a thing, then a person who has the belief is not, by virtue merely of *having* it, favorably disposed toward anything. Similarly for being unfavorably disposed toward a thing.

Another way to express the first premise is this: there is no belief such that a person who is in the state that consists in having the belief is, by virtue merely of being in the state, favorably or unfavorably disposed toward something.

Hume's second premise is: "morals . . . have an influence on the actions and affections . . . Morals excite passions, and produce or prevent actions." This, he says,

> is confirm'd by common experience, which informs us, that men are often govern'd by their duties, and are deter'd from some actions by the opinion of injustice, and impell'ed to others by that of obligation.

Thus people who are in the state we call "having a moral belief" are, by virtue merely of being in the state, favorably or unfavorably disposed toward something – perhaps an action, perhaps a person or state of affairs.

From Hume's two premises, it follows that the state we call "having a moral belief": is not properly called "having a moral *belief*": for one who is in the state we call "having a moral belief" is, by virtue merely of being in it, favorably or unfavorably disposed toward something, but there is no belief such that one who is in the state that consists in having the belief is, by virtue merely of being in it, favorably or unfavorably disposed toward something.

If we are not to call that state "having a moral belief," how is it to be described? Hume says: "To have the sense of virtue, is nothing but to *feel* a satisfaction of a particular kind from the contemplation of a character. The very *feeling* constitutes our praise or admiration." Or, as we might say: being in the state that we mistakenly call "having a moral belief" is merely having a favorable or unfavorable attitude – or, as I will for brevity put it, having a pro- or con-attitude. In short, then, we are to accept the No-Moral-Belief Thesis (IV).

From here it is only a short step to the rest of the Emotivist cluster. If what we mistakenly call having a moral belief is merely having an attitude, then asserting a moral sentence is not expressing a moral belief but merely displaying an attitude; hence the Speech-Act Thesis (III). If asserting a moral sentence is merely displaying an attitude, then it is not asserting anything with a truth-value; hence the No-Truth-Value Thesis (I). From that there straightway follows the remaining No-Fact-Thesis (II).

Should we accept Hume's argument for thesis (IV), and thereby for the rest of the Emotivist cluster?

7.3 We should be clear that any argument for Emotivism has a very heavy burden to carry.

Thesis (I) was very popular earlier in this century, but it is markedly less so nowadays: there are considerations that have emerged in recent years that make it seem highly implausible.

Consider, for example, the results of embedding moral sentences in longer sentences, such as, for example,

> If Alice ought to give Bert a banana, then there is someone who ought to give Bert a banana.

That should surely have a truth-value; in fact, it should surely be true – necessarily true at that. How is that possible, if its antecedent and consequent have no truth-values?

A related difficulty for thesis (I) issues from the fact that arguments such as the following should surely turn out to be valid:

> If Alice ought to give Bert a banana, then Alice ought to go to the grocery to buy some bananas,

Alice ought to give Bert a banana,
Therefore, Alice ought to go to the grocery to buy some
  bananas.

But how is that argument to be valid if "Alice ought to give Bert
a banana" and "Alice ought to go to the grocery to buy some
bananas" have no truth-values? A considerable amount of inge-
nuity has been invested in efforts to make out that arguments
such as this one can be, if not valid in the traditional sense, then
anyway 'valid', and to make out that being 'valid' is just as good
as being valid.[4] But surely the argument *is* valid in the traditional sense. What makes it valid is surely exactly the same
principle of logic – modus ponens – as the one that makes the
following argument valid:

If Alice gave Bert a banana, then Alice went to the grocery to
  buy some bananas,
Alice gave Bert a banana,
Therefore, Alice went to the grocery to buy some bananas.

A connected, more general, difficulty for thesis (I) lies in the
nature of truth itself. It is widely agreed that for an appropriately
constrained range of sentences, the results of replacing them for
the letter "S" in the schema (often called the disquotation
schema)

"S" is true if and only if S

are all true.[5] Thus "Snow is white" being in the range,

(1) "Snow is white" is true if and only if snow is white

---

[4] See, for example, Hare (1952), Blackburn (1984), Gibbard (1990). The difficulties I have been drawing attention to – to which those authors are responding – were first pointed to by Peter Geach in Geach (1965).
[5] The constraint excludes from the range of possible replacements for "S"
non-declarative sentences (such as "Go to the store!"), sentences (such as "I feel
hungry") which contain indexicals, sentences (such as "Schnee ist weiss") in a
foreign language, and certain others as well.

is true. Is there any good reason for excluding moral sentences from the range? Consider

(2) "Alice ought to give Bert a banana" is true if and only if Alice ought to give Bert a banana.

Surely (2) is every bit as plausible as (1) is. But the traditional account of the meaning of "if and only if" tells us that if (2) is true, then the two sentences that flank "if and only if" in it are either both true or both false; a fortiori, the sentence to the right of "if and only if" in (2) is itself either true or false. It follows that "Alice ought to give Bert a banana" does have a truth-value, and thesis (I) is false.

It is worth noticing, moreover, that it will do no better for a friend of thesis (I) to declare that (2) is false. The traditional account of the meaning of "if and only if" tells us that if (2) is false, then the two sentences that flank "if and only if" in it have different truth-values, one true and the other false; a fortiori, the sentence to the right of "if and only if" in (2) is itself either true or false. Indeed, the friend of thesis (I) must say that (2), though it is not itself a moral sentence, is – like moral sentences – itself neither true nor false.

These difficulties for thesis (I) are so serious that it is hard to imagine how any argument, whether Hume's or anyone else's, could plausibly be thought to lend weight to it.

7.4 It may be said that I have been unfair to Emotivism. I may be said to have focused on the letter of Emotivism, its cranky surface, and should instead have focused on its spirit, the deep and important idea that lies beneath the surface. Let us from here on use the name Letter-Emotivism to refer to the cluster of

---

A deflationary theory of truth is one that says, not merely that biconditionals such as I point to in the text above are true, but more strongly, that they exhaust what can be said about truth: such a theory says that there is nothing more to truth than the truth of those biconditionals. For a recent defense of a deflationary theory of truth, see Horwich (1990). It should be stressed, however, that the difficulty for thesis (I) that is pointed to in the text above does not arise only if a deflationary theory of truth is correct. Whether or not there is more to truth than the truth of those biconditionals, it is enough to make trouble for thesis (I) that biconditionals such as (2) are themselves true.

views I set out in section 7.1. What does the Spirit- Emotivist[6] say is cranky surface, and what does he say is the deep and important idea that lies beneath it?

He says that the No-Truth-Value Thesis (I) is part of the surface, and he rejects it, for the reasons I set out in the preceding section. Indeed, he does not merely say that moral sentences have truth-values, he says that some of them *are* true. For example, he says that torture is wrong; and it follows from torture's being wrong that the moral sentence "Torture is wrong" is true.

He says that the No-Fact Thesis (II) is also part of the surface. He says that there is nothing more to there being facts than there being true sentences; so since some moral sentences are true, it follows that there are moral facts.

He says that the Speech-Act Thesis (III) is also part of the surface. On his view, one who asserts a moral sentence does display an attitude, but he says that one who asserts a moral sentence also states something, true or false.

Lastly, he says that the No-Moral-Belief Thesis (IV) is also part of the surface. Of course that thesis won't do, he says. If Jones in all apparent sincerity asserts "Alice ought to give Bert a banana," then it may very well be true to say about him that he believes that Alice ought to give Bert a banana.

But if all four of the theses in Letter-Emotivism are surface, what's left that isn't surface?

What the Spirit-Emotivist would have us fix on is Hume's second premise. That, he says, expresses the deep and important idea beneath the cranky surface. It has led people to adopt Letter-Emotivism; it need not and should not have done.

Hume's second premise, in my summary of it above, says: people who are in the state we call "having a moral belief" are, by virtue merely of being in the state, favorably or unfavorably

---

[6] The person whose views I discuss in this section is an invented composite: see, for example, Harman (1977), Blackburn (1990), Stoljar (1993), and Horwich (1993)

I am indebted to Gilbert Harman for the information that Stevenson – a Letter-Emotivist in Stevenson (1945) – was the first to suggest that the spirit of Emotivism can be retained compatibly with rejecting thesis (I); see Stevenson (1963), pp. 214–20.

disposed toward something – perhaps an action, perhaps a person or state of affairs. The Spirit-Emotivist says that this is wholly right. But he rejects Hume's first premise, which says that that there is no belief of which this is true. He says that we should not take Hume's second premise to be part of an argument for the conclusion that there are no moral beliefs; we should instead take it to supply us with an account of what having a moral belief *is*. The deep and important idea, then, is this:

(IV*) Belief-Attitude Thesis: There is such a thing as having a moral belief, but a person's having a moral belief *is* the person's having an attitude, pro or con.[7]

No wonder, then, that in asserting a moral sentence one displays an attitude – though one also states something true or false.

This idea is worth taking a closer look at.

7.5 Why so? Not, I think, because if we accept the Belief-Attitude Thesis (IV*) we are thereby committed to Moral Scepticism. Suppose Smith believes that Alice ought to give Bert a banana. The fact (supposing it a fact) that Smith's believing that Alice ought to give Bert a banana is Smith's having a pro-attitude toward Alice's giving Bert a banana is entirely compatible with Smith's having evidence for his belief; indeed, it is entirely compatible with Smith's having a proof of his belief.

---

[7] Huw Price calls accepting thesis (IV) "retreat to the head", and draws attention to the similarities between retreat to the head in ethics and retreat to the head in other areas of philosophy; he himself recommends accepting (IV*) instead. See Price (1988).

Gilbert Harman says that what I am calling Spirit-Emotivism

is not completely trivial; it does make one good point. To think that something is a good thing, the right thing to do, what ought to be done, and so on, are ways of being in favor of something, and to think that something is a bad thing, the wrong thing to do, what ought not to be done, and so on, are ways of being against something. (Harman (1977, p. 52)

The thesis does tell us that Smith did not acquire the belief until he acquired the pro-attitude (and vice versa). But that leaves open that he came to have the belief, and thus the pro-attitude, for good enough reason to count as having found out that the belief is true.

Since what we are interested in is threats to moral objectivity, we can therefore bypass Spirit-Emotivism; and readers are cordially invited to skip straightway to chapter 8.

But I think that Spirit-Emotivism is not merely not a deep and important idea, but a mistake – a mistake that issues largely from failing to take the richness of moral thinking seriously enough – and since it is currently very popular, I take the liberty of stopping to bring out some of the difficulties it faces.

7.6 We should begin by becoming clear about what the Belief-Attitude Thesis (IV*) says. Suppose Smith believes that Alice ought to give Bert a banana; his believing this is a mental state, and let us call it SMITH-BELIEF. The Spirit- Emotivist tells us that there is a mental state SMITH-PRO-ATTITUDE that consists in Smith's having a pro-attitude toward Alice's giving Bert a banana, and that SMITH-BELIEF is identical with SMITH-PRO-ATTITUDE.

Now it seems an odd idea that a mental state which is a believing could *be* a mental state which is a having of a pro-attitude. And indeed, for very many believings and havings of pro-attitudes, this surely can't be the case. Consider Jones, who believes that Tom will win the election in November. Call his having that belief JONES-BELIEF. Suppose Jones has a pro- attitude toward Tom's winning the election in November. Call his having that pro-attitude JONES-PRO-ATTITUDE. Can we say that JONES-BELIEF *is* JONES-PRO-ATTITUDE? Not if we suppose that JONES-BELIEF is essentially a believing that Tom will win, and that JONES-PRO-ATTITUDE is essentially a having of a pro-attitude toward Tom's winning. For suppose that JONES-BELIEF *is* JONES-PRO-ATTITUDE. Then any possible world in which the one exists, the other exists; thus every possible world in which Jones believes that Tom will win is a world in which he has a pro-attitude toward Tom's winning. But that won't do at all. Jones could have believed that Tom will win while lacking a pro-attitude toward Tom's winning.

What makes trouble for the identification of believing with having a pro-attitude in Jones's case is clear enough. Jones believes that Tom will win. So the content of his belief is: that Tom will win. Jones has a pro-attitude toward Tom's winning. So the content of his pro-attitude is: that Tom will win. So the content of his belief is the same as the content of his pro-attitude. But for whatever content you choose, it is possible to have a belief with that content while lacking a pro-attitude with that content.

Quite generally, then, we cannot identify a mental state which is a believing with a mental state which is a having of a pro-attitude if the content of the belief is the same as the content of the pro-attitude.

On the other hand, we cannot identify a mental state which is a believing with a mental state which is a having of a pro-attitude unless the content of the belief and the content of the pro-attitude bear some close relation to each other – else it would be possible for the believing to exist without the having of the pro-attitude. What is this close relation?

What is this close relation, for the particular case of moral beliefs? I can think of only two possible answers.

According to the first, we are to rewrite moral sentences in such a way that the moral term in them appears prefixed to a nonmoral referring expression. For example, we are to rewrite "Alice ought to give Bert a banana" as

Ought (Alice's giving Bert a banana),

and "Alice ought not give Bert a banana" as

Ought-Not (Alice's giving Bert a banana).

There are moral sentences that do not contain "ought" and "ought not", for example, sentences such as "Alice is just" and "Alice is brave". Presumably we are to rewrite them as

Just (Alice),

and

Brave (Alice).

And similarly for such sentences as "Alice is unjust" and "Alice is a coward."

Then we are to say that believing a moral sentence is having the attitude indicated or expressed by the prefix toward the thing – state of affairs or person or act or government, whatever it may be – that is referred to by the referring expression. Thus believing that X ought to do alpha is having the Ought-pro-attitude toward the state of affairs that consists in X's doing alpha; believing that X is just is having the Just-pro-attitude toward X; believing that X is brave is having the Brave- pro-attitude toward X; and so on.

A Spirit-Emotivist who takes this first line may then say that the trouble that faced identification in Jones's case does not face identification in Smith's. There is no possible world in which Smith believes that X ought to do alpha while lacking the Ought-pro-attitude toward X's doing alpha; there is no possible world in which Smith believes that X is just while lacking the Just-pro-attitude toward X; and so on. And if those states are necessary accompaniments of each other, why not identify them?

But we need to ask: what are the Ought-pro-attitude, the Just-pro-attitude, and the Brave-pro-attitude? *What* pro-attitudes are indicated or expressed by these prefixes "Ought," "Just," and "Brave"?[8]

"Pro-attitude*s*": plural, since they had presumably better be distinct. Certainly the Just-pro-attitude can't be identical with the Brave-pro-attitude if believing that Alice is just is to be

---

[8] A further difficulty issues from the existence of such sentences as "Alice needn't give Bert a banana." How are we to rewrite them? "Needn't (Alice's giving Bert a banana)"? What attitude is expressed by *that* prefix? Or is "Alice needn't give Bert a banana" not a moral sentence at all? (But am I not, in asserting it, asserting that morality permits Alice to not give Bert a banana?) Emotivists typically focus on "ought" and "ought not," and ignore the likes of "needn't," "all right," and "okay" – as well as the likes of "just" and "brave," which I invite attention to in the text above and below.

having the Just-pro-attitude toward Alice, and believing that Alice is brave is to be having the Brave-pro-attitude toward Alice – else believing that Alice is just and believing that Alice is brave would be having one and the same pro-attitude toward one and the same entity (Alice), and thus believing that Alice is just would be identical with believing that Alice is brave, which is patently false. And it is hard to see what could mark the Ought-pro-attitude as identical with one but not the other of the Just-pro-attitude and the Brave-pro-attitude.

So let us suppose that the Spirit-Emotivist who takes this line would say that the Ought-pro-attitude, the Just-pro-attitude, and the Brave-pro-attitude are three distinct pro-attitudes.[9]

Are there three distinct pro-attitudes, one of which you have whenever you believe X ought to do alpha, another of which you have whenever you believe X is just, and the third of which you have whenever you believe X is brave?

Is it even so much as the case that whenever you believe that a person ought to do a thing you have *a* pro-attitude – let alone the same one on every such occasion? Or whenever you believe that a person is just or brave? When I believe that Alice ought to do a thing, I may hope she will do it. Or I may feel pleased at the thought of her doing it. But mightn't I have no pro-attitude at all toward her doing it? (Mightn't I just wonder whether she will do it? Or just feel resentful at her not having already done it? Or have no interest in the matter at all?) But if we don't always have *a* pro-attitude whenever we have beliefs of these three kinds, then a fortiori we don't always have one pro-attitude whenever we have a belief of the one kind, and a second whenever we have a belief of the second kind, and a third whenever we have a belief of the third kind.

There is *a* way – I think there is only one way – of securing that whenever we have such beliefs we do have pro-attitudes, and indeed, that the pro-attitudes differ. Well, not exactly that the pro-attitudes differ, for it says nothing about what they are, but anyway that havings of the pro-attitudes differ.

---

[9] Compare the passage I quoted from Harman in footnote 7: Harman there said that moral beliefs are "ways" – plural – of being for or against something.

What I have in mind is that the Spirit-Emotivist can say he is not talking about phenomenologically distinguishable pro-attitudes. But (he can say) you do quite certainly have the Ought-, Just-, and Brave-pro-attitudes whenever you have beliefs of the three kinds. For having the Ought-pro-attitude toward X's doing alpha *just is* believing that X ought to do alpha, and having the Just-pro-attitude toward X *just is* believing that X is just, and having the Brave-pro-attitude toward X *just is* believing that X is brave.

If the Spirit-Emotivist proceeds in this way, he guarantees that you have the Ought-pro-attitude toward X's doing alpha whenever you believe that X ought to do alpha, and that you have the Just-pro-attitude toward X whenever you believe that X is just, and that you have the Brave-pro-attitude toward X whenever you believe that X is brave. Moreover, he guarantees that having the Ought-pro-attitude toward X's doing alpha is different from having the Just-pro-attitude toward X, and that both of those are different from having the Brave-pro-attitude toward X – for believing that X ought to do alpha, and believing that X is just, and believing that X is brave, are on any view different mental states.

If the Spirit-Emotivist does proceed in this way, however, he makes the thesis he presented us with be uninformative. He told us that believing that X ought to do alpha is having the Ought-pro-attitude toward X's doing alpha. We asked: what is that Ought-pro-attitude? He replied: don't worry, having the Ought-pro-attitude toward X's doing alpha just is believing that X ought to do alpha. What have we learned, then? Nothing at all! Similarly for what he told us about about believing that X is just and believing that X is brave.

In sum, the Spirit-Emotivist's thesis seemed dubious. He can secure its truth, but only by making it uninformative.

It may be said that *that* way of laying out the required close relation between belief and pro-attitude was, after all, a silly one. So let us turn to the second possibility. Instead of rewriting a moral sentence in such a way that the very moral term in it appears as a prefix, the Spirit-Emotivist may say that we are to divide moral sentences into the favorable (those with, as it were, positive valence) and the unfavorable (those with, as it were negative valence), and rewrite the former as expressions of the form

Pro (. . .)

and the latter as expressions of the form

Con (. . .),

in which the dots are filled in with some nonmoral referring expression. Thus, for example, "Alice ought to give Bert a banana" being favorable, and "Alice ought not give Bert a banana" being unfavorable, we are to rewrite them as

Pro (Alice's giving Bert a banana)

and

Con (Alice's giving Bert a banana)

respectively.

Then we are to say that believing a favorable moral sentence is having the attitude indicated or expressed by the prefix "Pro" toward the thing referred to by the referring expression, and believing an unfavorable moral sentence is having the attitude indicated or expressed by the prefix "Con" toward the thing referred to by the referring expression.

The Spirit-Emotivist who takes this second line seems to have an easier life than the Spirit-Emotivist who takes the first. There pretty plainly are such attitudes as approval and disapproval, and one could hardly complain of a difficulty in distinguishing between them: approval and disapproval are on any view distinct.

Moreover, I asked: is it even so much as the case that whenever you believe that a person ought to do a thing you have *a* pro-attitude – let alone the same one on every such occasion? And I asked: mightn't I believe that Alice ought to do a thing and have no pro-attitude at all toward her doing it? The Spirit-Emotivist can say No. He can say: no doubt you needn't hope she will do it, or feel pleased at the thought of her doing it. You needn't have any phenomenologically detectable interest in the matter. But you must at least approve of her doing it. After all, what you believe is that she *ought* to do it; and how could you believe that without approving of her doing it?

But life isn't really easier for the Spirit-Emotivist who takes this second line. In the first place, while approval and disapproval are on any view distinct, the Spirit-Emotivist needs to avail himself of a special kind of approval and disapproval: these have to be moral approval and moral disapproval. For presumably he does not wish to say that believing Alice ought to do a thing is having toward her doing it the same attitude of approval that I have toward the sound of your splendid new violin. The problem I point to here is a familiar one; Hume discussed it, and so did some contemporary Emotivists. It pays to stress its seriousness, however. For if there is no way of saying what the attitude of moral approval consists in other than by saying that having it toward a thing *just is* believing a favorable moral sentence, then this Spirit-Emotivist's thesis is uninformative – like that of the Spirit-Emotivist who takes the first line, and secures its truth in the way I indicated.[10]

Another difficulty is at least as serious. How are we to find, for every moral sentence, a nonmoral referring expression to replace the three dots? It may seem plausible enough that we can rewrite "Alice ought to give Bert a banana" as "Pro (Alice's giving Bert a banana)", but how on earth are we to rewrite "Alice is just" and "Alice is brave"? They cannot both be rewritten as

Pro (Alice):

the belief that Alice is just and the belief that Alice is brave cannot both be identified with the having of one and the same favorable attitude toward one and the same thing, namely

[10] A further difficulty is the analogue of the one I mentioned in footnote 8. *Are all moral sentences divisible into the favorable or unfavorable?* What of "Alice needn't give Bert a banana"? (I can certainly believe that without either approving or disapproving of Alice's giving Bert a banana.) Or is it not a moral sentence at all?

Alice, for the belief that Alice is just is not identical with the belief that Alice is brave. Nor, for the same reason, can they both be rewritten as

Pro (Alice's character).

Therefore more complex replacements for the three dots are required. I see no even remotely plausible candidates.

This difficulty that faces the Spirit-Emotivist who takes the second line is analogous to the difficulty I drew attention to in responding to the Spirit-Emotivist who takes the first line. The Spirit-Emotivist who takes the first line must find an account of the many different specific pro- and con-attitudes a, b, c, and so on, such that having a moral belief is having one or other of them toward something. The Spirit-Emotivist who takes the second line must find an account of the many different entities a′, b′, c′, and so on, such that having a moral belief is having either the general pro- or the general con-attitude toward one or other of them. These two difficulties are two sides of the same coin; both issue from the Spirit-Emotivist's insufficient appreciation of the richness of moral thought – the fact that we have many different kinds of moral belief. It seems to me that the prospect of supplying either one of the required accounts is most kindly describable as dim.

It should be noticed that the problems I point to here are not faced only by the Spirit-Emotivist: the Letter-Emotivist faces them too. If you think that having a moral belief is having an attitude, then you have to tell us which attitude toward what in the case of this moral belief and which attitude toward what in the case of that one. But so also: if you think that there is no such thing as having a moral belief, and that a person who is mistakenly described as having a moral belief really only has an attitude, then you have to tell us which attitude toward what a person has who is mistakenly described as having this moral belief and which attitude toward what a person has who is mistakenly described as having that one.

7.7 A further difficulty emerges if the Spirit-Emotivist accepts yet another popular thesis.

I said it was Hume's second premise that the Spirit-Emotivist would have us fix on, and in my summary of it, it says: people who are in the state we call "having a moral belief" are, by virtue merely of being in the state, favorably or unfavorably disposed toward something – perhaps an action, perhaps a person or state of affairs. I therefore took the Spirit-Emotivist to accept

> (IV*) Belief-Attitude Thesis: There is such a thing as having a moral belief, but a person's having a moral belief *is* the person's having an attitude, pro or con.

But there is another way in which Hume's second premise is often summarized. Here again are Hume's own words: "morals . . . have an influence on the actions and affections . . . Morals excite passions, and produce or prevent actions." This, Hume said,

> is confirm'd by common experience, which informs us, that men are often govern'd by their duties, and are deter'd from some actions by the opinion of injustice, and impell'ed to others by that of obligation.

Some people have summarized this idea in the words: moral beliefs have motivating force – they motivate people to act. Now thesis (IV*) says nothing at all about action, so there appears to be a new thesis in the offing here, which a Spirit-Emotivist might accept as well.

But what exactly does the new thesis say? Do people who say "Moral beliefs have motivating force – they motivate people to act" mean that *all* moral beliefs motivate people to act? That seems intuitively an odd idea. If I believe that Alice ought to give Bert a banana, I may be motivated to tell Alice to give Bert a banana. Or to tell Bert to sue if she doesn't. But I certainly need not be motivated to do those things. Intuitively, it seems to be entirely possible that I am not motivated do anything at all relevant to Alice's giving Bert a banana.

Whether or not they mean that all moral beliefs motivate, it seems clear that they do at least mean that certain first-person moral beliefs motivate. Thus, for example, that my believing that *I* ought to give Bert a banana motivates me to act. To act how? To give Bert a banana, I suppose. (Notice the immediate availability of an answer to "To act how?" in the case of first-person moral beliefs, by contrast with the case of third-person moral beliefs.) More generally, for any man X,

> X's believing that X ought to do alpha motivates him to do alpha.

That anyway seems to have a better chance of being true than the quite general thesis that all moral beliefs motivate.

We should be clear that people who accept this idea have something strong in mind. Thus it might be said that any number of kinds of beliefs may motivate, and in the case of many beliefs perhaps always do, and thus that there is nothing special about moral beliefs in this respect. Consider breadbox beliefs: beliefs about breadboxes. It might be said that they too motivate. Suppose X believes that his opening his breadbox will or would scare away the mouse in it. X's having this belief might motivate him to open his breadbox. No doubt X's having this belief doesn't *by itself* motivate him to open his breadbox: no doubt X's having this belief motivates him to open his breadbox only given a background of his wanting to scare away the mouse in it. But I doubt that our use of "motivates" is so strict as to allow of saying that a person's having a certain belief motivates him to act only where the person's having the belief by itself motivates him to act. So let us make clear that that is what is being claimed here about moral beliefs. Thus the thesis before us is intended to say:

> (V*) Motivation Thesis: X's believing that X ought to do alpha by itself motivates him to do alpha.

We have not yet fully brought out how strong the thesis here is. A widely accepted and very plausible theory about motivation – it comes down to us from Hume himself – tells us that X's believing that his doing alpha will or would have a certain feature F motivates him to do alpha only if X wants to do something F-ish. (For example, X's believing that his opening his breadbox will or would scare away the mouse in it motivates him to open his breadbox only if he wants to scare away the mouse in it.) So X's believing that his doing alpha will or would have a certain feature F *by itself* motivates him to do alpha only if it contains his wanting to do something F-ish. In particular, X's believing that he ought to do alpha *by itself* motivates him to do alpha only if it contains his wanting to do what he ought to do. Suppose we accept that widely accepted and very plausible theory about motivation. (It is hard to see how we could reasonably reject it.) Then (V*) is true only if

> (VI*) Wants Thesis: X's believing that X ought to do alpha contains his wanting to do what he ought to do

is true. On any view, (VI*) is a strong thesis.

How could a mental state that consists in believing something 'contain' wanting to do something? Well, says a friend of these ideas, that is what is special about moral believings. They (unlike breadbox believings) do not motivate only given a background want: they themselves contain the want.

Let us return now to the Spirit-Emotivist. He accepts (IV*). He *may* also accept (V*). If he does, he is committed to (VI*) as well.

It is worth noticing that the appropriate word here really is "may," and not "must," for there is no contradiction in the Spirit-Emotivist if he accepts (IV*) and rejects (V*). I am sure that many Spirit-Emotivists would say that (V*) is a consequence of (IV*). Indeed, I am sure that many people who are attracted to (IV*) are attracted to (IV*) precisely because they think that moral beliefs motivate, and that if moral beliefs consist in the havings of pro-attitudes, that would tidily explain how come they motivate. But it is worth noticing that a Spirit-Emotivist can consistently accept (IV*) and reject (V*). Let us see how.

In accepting (IV*), the Spirit-Emotivist accepts

(1) X's believing that X ought to do alpha is X's having the appropriate pro-attitude toward his doing alpha.

Which is the appropriate pro-attitude? Well, perhaps it is the specific Ought-pro-attitude. Perhaps it is the general attitude of moral approval. No matter for present purposes. If the Spirit-Emotivist also accepts.

(2) X's having the appropriate pro-attitude toward his doing alpha by itself motivates him to do alpha

then of course he is committed to (V*) as well as (IV*). But he need not accept (2). The Spirit-Emotivist *can* say that X's having the appropriate pro-attitude toward his doing alpha may or may not motivate him to do alpha, and if it does, it does not do so by itself: if it does, it does so only given a background of X's wanting to do what he ought to do. That is, the want is not contained in the belief-which-is-a-pro-attitude but may (or may not) accompany it.

In one way, this is an unattractive line for a Spirit-Emotivist to take. For if the Spirit-Emotivist says that X's having the appropriate pro-attitude toward his doing alpha motivates him to do alpha only given a background of X's wanting to do what he ought to do, then the following question arises: what is the gain for the Spirit-Emotivist in identifying X's believing that X ought to do alpha with X's having the appropriate pro-attitude toward his doing alpha? What's the interest for the Spirit-Emotivist in thesis (IV*)?

On the other hand, this line has its attractions for him. There are any number of more familiar pro-attitudes – more familiar than the specific Ought-pro-attitude or the general attitude of moral approval – which motivate only given a background want. Suppose I admire your new Mercedes. That may or may not motivate me to do something. Perhaps it motivates me to ask you for a ride. Perhaps it motivates me to throw a brick through the windshield. (Let's not forget about the existence of jealousy and malice.) But if it motivates me to do anything, it does so only given a background of my wanting something, as it might be, to have a ride in an admirable car, or to do you a harm. Why not say the same of the way in which the moral pro-attitude(s) motivate?

Moreover, the Spirit-Emotivist says that my believing that Alice ought to give Bert a banana and my believing that I ought to give Bert a banana both consist in my having one and the same pro-attitude, but toward different objects: in the former case toward Alice's giving Bert a banana, in the latter case toward my doing so. Now as I said, it is an intuitively odd idea that my believing that Alice ought to give Bert a banana must motivate me to act. So the Spirit-Emotivist has three options. He can say (i) so much the worse for intuition: my having the pro-attitude toward an object by itself motivates me to act, whether the object is Alice's giving Bert a banana, or my giving Bert a banana. Or he can say (ii) my having the pro-attitude toward the one object does not by itself motivate me to act but my having it toward the other does. Thus whether having (one and the same) pro-attitude toward different objects by itself motivates turns on what the object is. Or he can say (iii) my having the pro-attitude toward an object never by itself motivates me to act, no matter what the object is: it motivates (if it does) only given a background want. This is the line I have been pointing to the possibility of; a Spirit-Emotivist might well find it the most attractive of the three options.

Finally, the Spirit-Emotivist had really better steer clear of (V*) in any case, even at the cost of swallowing that (IV*) is a less interesting thesis than might have appeared. That is because (V*) is true only if (VI*) is, and (VI*) is at best dubious, and requires for its truth something that the *Spirit-Emotivist* cannot consistently accept. So let us have a closer look at (VI*).

7.8 I said just above that

> (VI*) Wants Thesis: X's believing that X ought to do alpha contains his wanting to do what he ought to do

is at best dubious. I don't have in mind by way of objection to it that people who believe they ought to do a thing don't always do it. Of course they don't. But (VI*) doesn't say they do. It says only that people who believe they ought to do a thing want to do what they ought to do, which is compatible with their wanting more strongly to do something else instead. Accepting (VI*) requires accepting only that the believer in a measure wants to do what he ought to do, not that he overwhelmingly, or even very much, wants to do what he ought to do.

I also don't have in mind by way of objection to (VI*) that people sometimes believe they ought to do a thing and do not want to do it. Indeed, do not *at all* want to do it. I believe I ought to pay my income tax; I am sure I am not unique among those who share this belief in never once having wanted to pay it. But (VI*) does not say that X's believing that X ought to do alpha contains his wanting to do alpha; what it says is contained in X's believing is, rather, his wanting to do what he ought to do. That is different.

Perhaps some analogies will help bring out the difference. You might believe that becoming rich requires you to do a great many things: get to work on time, refrain from idling during working hours, keep your fingernails clean, and so on. You might want to do at most some but not others of these things. But that is compatible with your all the same wanting to become rich.

Again, you might believe that prevailing law says you must do a great many things: pay your income tax, park your car only in such and such places, refrain from littering, and so on. You might want to do at most some but not others of these things. But that is compatible with your all the same wanting to act as the law says you must.

So similarly, you might believe that you ought to do a great many things: pay your income tax, keep your promises, refrain from causing pain, and so on. You might want to do at most some but not others of these things. But that is compatible with your all the same wanting to do what you ought to do.

It is only that want – your wanting to do what you ought to do – which thesis (VI*) says is contained in your believing that you ought to do a thing.

The trouble is that there certainly *seem* to be people who from time to time believe they ought to do a thing without wanting, at that time, to do what they ought to do. Here is Jones, seated by the fire, reading a novel. He says he believes he ought to go out and shovel the snow off his sidewalk. But he also says that he not only does not at all want to go out and shovel the snow, he does not at all now want to do what he ought to do. Intuitively, at all events, it seems to be entirely possible for both of Jones' two reports about himself to be true. Accepting (VI*) requires supposing that they cannot both be true. How is that to be made out?

The friend of (VI*) might reason as follows. Suppose we accept that Jones really does believe he ought to shovel the snow. Then mustn't we suppose that he feels a twinge of disappointment, a twinge of discomfort, a certain unease? Perhaps these feelings are very slight, and easily overcome if the novel is a good one. Perhaps Jones is unaccustomed to having such feelings, and hence did not notice or recognize them. But if he does really believe he ought to shovel the snow, then it must be that he does have those feelings, and thus does in a measure want, if not to shovel the snow, then anyway to do what he ought to do.

Alternatively, suppose we accept that Jones neither wants to shovel the snow nor wants to be doing what he ought. Then mustn't we suppose that he has only an inverted commas belief that he ought to shovel the snow? – that is, a belief that others believe he ought to?

But why, after all, should we agree?

Something is at work in people who accept

(VI*) Wants Thesis: X's believing that X ought to do alpha contains his wanting to do what he ought to do.

What it is emerges if we look at what is at work in people who accept a certain weaker thesis, namely:

(VII*) Weak Wants Thesis: There cannot be a person who has a fully fleshed-out body of moral beliefs like thine and mine but who never wants to do what he ought to do.

It should be clear in any case that (VI*) is not true unless (VII*) is.

7.9 What might incline a person to accept the Weak Wants Thesis (VII*)?

If there were people who have moral beliefs but who never want to do what they ought to do, what would they be like? Since they never want to do what they ought to do, their believing that they ought to do a thing does not contain the want to do what they ought to do. More strongly, their believing that they ought to do a thing is never even accompanied by the want to do what they ought to do. It follows that their believing that they ought to do a thing never motivates them to do the thing. More generally, their moral beliefs have no affect on their actions.

That is compatible with their very often doing what they believe they ought to do. On the one hand, there may be things alpha such that they believe they ought to do alpha and also want to do alpha. On the other hand, there may be things alpha such that they believe they ought to do alpha, and, while not wanting to do alpha, need to do alpha if they are to do or get something else that they want.

For example, Chilly (as I'll call him) cares only about the members of his immediate family, and Very Chilly cares about no one but himself. We may suppose at least this much about both of them: they want the trust and respect of their neighbors, these being very valuable things to have in the long run. So where it is not very costly to do so, and where their doing so is visible by others, they do what they believe they ought to do in order to earn them.

Moreover, such people needn't be chilly. Warm (as I'll call him) cares about some people outside his own immediate family, and Very Warm cares about everyone. (Cry in the vicinity of Very Warm, and he'll lend you his shoulder despite your being a total stranger.) These two don't want merely the fruits of doing what they believe they ought to do; there are things – acts of kindness toward others – that they both believe they ought to do and want to do. It should be stressed about them, however, that when they do those acts of kindness, that is *only* because they want to do them (or want the fruits of doing them, for small kindnesses do sometimes bear fruit). They wouldn't do the things if they didn't have those wants.

Are these people possible? There is something at a minimum odd about them.[11] They never want to do what they ought; we might well ask how come they acquired beliefs about what they ought to do in the first place.

An obvious first answer is that acquiring such beliefs is useful. Trouble descends on people who do what they ought not do. And, as I said, doing what one ought to do may well buy one trust and respect.

But isn't it enough for avoiding trouble and obtaining trust and respect that one act as others believe one ought to act? Isn't it therefore enough for avoiding the one and obtaining the other that one have acquired inverted commas moral beliefs? If my four characters are to be possible they have to have acquired, not merely beliefs about what others believe they ought to do, but beliefs (all simply) about what they ought to do.

This point is worth stress. Take Chilly, for example. (Any one of my four would have done as well.) For Chilly to be possible, there has to be for him (as there is for us), a difference between the question whether others believe he ought to do alpha and the question whether he ought to do alpha. And it has to be possible for him to believe that what others believe about what he ought to do is correct or is mistaken.

But given Chilly has arrived at the belief that others believe he ought to do alpha, what could be the point or interest for him in asking himself whether their belief is correct or is mistaken? For him, the point or interest in this further question has to be purely theoretical: if he is to be supposed to ask himself this further question, we have to think of him as asking it out of mere idle curiosity. That would certainly be an odd business.

But an impossible business? People who accept the Weak Wants Thesis (VII*) need, not merely that this would be odd, but that it is impossible. How is that to be made out?

---

[11] David Brink describes the person he calls "the amoralist" as "unmoved" by, "indifferent to" what he believes to be morality's demands on him; see Brink (1989). I think this leaves open that his amoralist is any one of my four characters or anything in between. Brink believes that the possibility of his amoralist is a datum, from which we can argue against theories of the kind we are looking at; I don't believe it is a *datum*, though I think such people possible. Moreover, I think he underestimates their oddity.

Most of us do sometimes indulge in idle curiosity. A New Englan-
der might wonder, idly, whether Californians (like New Englanders)
prefer brown eggs to white. Or one might wonder, idly, whether
beavers would eat chocolate pudding if offered it. If we don't care
about the answers, we don't *dwell* on the questions, and don't try
hard to find answers to them. But we do sometimes wonder about
them, and sometimes form views about their answers.

What I suggest is at work in anyone who accepts the Weak
Wants Thesis (VII*) is the idea that moral curiosity is different,
and indeed different in the following way. If you wonder
whether Californians prefer brown eggs to white, you are wondering about a matter of fact; and if you conclude that they do,
your conclusion has a content, and is true or false. So even if
you don't care whether your conclusion is true, it is true or
false. By contrast – so I take anyone who accepts (VII*) to
believe – a person who wonders whether he ought to do alpha
is not wondering about anything with a content, and hence is
not really wondering about anything, and his concluding that
he ought to do alpha is not his drawing any conclusion with a
content, and hence is not really his concluding anything. That
says what is *not* going on in a person who wonders whether he
ought to do alpha and then concludes that he ought to do alpha.
What *is* going on in him? His wondering is his canvassing
considerations that might (or might not) issue in his having the
appropriate pro-attitude toward doing alpha, and his concluding is merely his coming to have it. So if a person never has that
pro-attitude toward anything, he uses the word "ought" with no
meaning at all.[12]

---

[12] Gibbard invites us to imagine that we are two people who do not care
whether we act as we ought but who have (putatively) arrived at different
answers to the question whether it would be wrong to do such and such. And
Gibbard asks: "in what do we disagree? Is it just in the application of a word? . . .
What's at stake in whether you convince me? Aren't we just going through the
forms of a moral dispute, using the word 'wrong' with no meaning?" (Gibbard,
1993, p. 319) It would of course be hard to imagine two such people (Chilly and
Warm?) disputing about their different answers, since disputes don't normally
arise between two people who don't care which side is right; and by hypothesis,
nothing is at stake for either party in whether his own or the other fellow's view
is correct. But to conclude that the parties use the word "wrong" with no
meaning is to rely on the assumption that the meaning of "wrong" is exhausted
by its link with the appropriate attitudes.

In short, "I ought . . . ," unlike "Californians prefer . . . ," lacks a truth-value: its meaning is exhausted by its use to express the appropriate pro-attitude, and it is used without meaning by a person who never has the appropriate pro-attitude.

In shorter still, what is at work in anyone who accepts (VII*) is Letter-Emotivism.

Moreover, (VII*) is not true unless Letter-Emotivism is true. Making a case for (VII*) requires making out that there is no such thing as purely theoretical, purely idle curiosity about whether so and so ought to do such and such. Making that out requires making out that sentences of the form "X ought to do alpha" have no truth-value – else it could perfectly well be the question what their truth-value *is* that one is purely theoretically, purely idly curious about.

Let us go back to the Spirit-Emotivist, then. The Spirit-Emotivist accepts

> (IV*) Belief-Attitude Thesis: There is such a thing as having a moral belief, but a person's having a moral belief *is* the person's having an attitude, pro or con.

I said he *may* also accept

> (V*) Motivation Thesis: X's believing that X ought to do alpha by itself motivates him to do alpha.

Given the theory about motivation I pointed to, (V*) is true only if

> (VI*) Wants Thesis: X's believing that X ought to do alpha contains his wanting to do what he ought to do

is true. Now (VI*) is true only if

(VII*) Weak Wants Thesis: There cannot be a person who has a fully fleshed-out body of moral beliefs like thine and mine but who never wants to do what he ought to do

is true. But (VII*) is true only if Letter-Emotivism is true. Therefore, as I said, the Spirit-Emotivist had really better steer clear of the Motivation Thesis (V*). And so should we.

Even if we reject (V*), however, it remains the case that my four characters are, if not impossible, then very unlikely. They are mentally divided in a curious way. By hypothesis, each has a full-fledged body of beliefs about what he ought to do; but by hypothesis also, in the case of each, his beliefs are sealed off from, or float free of, everything else in his life that bears on the choices he makes. Their moral beliefs, unlike ours, never impinge on what they do: their moral beliefs are pure epiphenomena. I suggested in the preceding chapter that moral facts are epiphenomenal; it would be quite another thing, and a very odd thing, for all of a man's moral beliefs to be epiphenomenal too.

7.10 In the case of most if not all of us, our moral beliefs are not epiphenomenal. We often do things we want to do *both* because we want to do them *and* because we believe we ought to and want to do what we ought. (Much of what we believe we ought to do we are inclined to do by mere ordinary fellow-feeling.) On other occasions, we do things we do not want to do, and do them because we believe we ought to and want to do what we ought.

Making out that our moral beliefs are non-epiphenomenal does not require making out that our believing we ought to do a thing contains our having wants – just as making out that our breadbox beliefs, or our beliefs about impressionist paintings or anything else, are non-epiphenomenal does not require making out that our having those beliefs contains our having wants. It is our (independently) having the relevant wants that makes the beliefs *be* non-epiphenomenal. Hume said that "men are often govern'd by their duties, and are deter'd from some actions by the opinion of injustice, and impell'ed to others by that of obligation." Yes, but that is because duty, justice, and obligation matter to most of us.

There are other ways in which wants figure in moral beliefs, or anyway in their content. Or so I think, and will suggest in the following chapter.

8

Evaluatives and Directives

8.1 One reason – I think it may be the main reason – why the crack in the universe of discourse between the moral and the nonmoral seems to be so deep is that we have three connected ideas. First, and fundamental, we think that there is such a property as being good, or goodness, and that there is such a property as being bad, or badness. Second, we think that there therefore is such a relation as being better than, or betterness. Third, we think that all moral sentences are analyzable into sentences of the forms "X is good" or "X is bad" or "X is better than Y" by the assertion of which we predicate the properties goodness or badness or the relation betterness; thus all of morality reduces ultimately to the properties goodness and badness and the relation betterness. Once you have accepted the first of these ideas, the others seem very plausible, and the first itself seems very pausible. Let us see why they do, and then see how accepting them makes moral objectivity seem to be a fantasy.

Is there such a property as goodness? G. E. Moore thought it obvious that there is. After all, some things are good and others are not, and surely it follows that there is a property – the property goodness – that all and only good things have in common.[1] Similar reasoning yields that there is such a property as badness.

---

[1] Moore said: Ethics is

> undoubtedly concerned with the question what good conduct is; but, being concerned with this, it obviously does not start at the beginning, unless it is prepared to tell us

If you think that there is such a property as goodness, you would find it very natural to think that there is such a relation as being better than, or betterness. You would find it very natural to think that every good thing has this relation to everything that is not good, and indeed, that for every pair of things X and Y, either X has it to Y, or Y has it to X, or neither has it to the other, X and Y being equally good or equally bad or neither good nor bad. That there is such a relation does not follow *just* from there being such a property as goodness. Moore invited us to agree that there is such a property as being yellow, and there is no reason to think he supposed that there is such a relation as being more yellow than. But it would be very natural to think that being good had better have a comparative, and Moore himself plainly thought it did.

Suppose we accept both of these ideas. Then the third also seems very plausible. Asserting "Alice is good" is predicating the property goodness, asserting "The government of Badland is bad" is predicating the property badness, asserting "The state of affairs Charles wants to bring about is better than the state of affairs David wants to bring about" is predicating the relation betterness.

Asserting such sentences as those is making moral assessments of entities that are not human acts; what of moral sentences by the assertion of which we say that morality requires a person to do this or that? Given that there is such a relation as betterness, it follows that whenever a person, say Alice, is confronted with a choice between doing alpha or not doing alpha, either her doing alpha would be better than her not doing alpha, or her not doing alpha would be better than her doing alpha, or neither would be better than the other. If neither would be better than the other, then surely it can make

---

what is good as well as what is conduct. For 'good conduct' is a complex notion: all conduct is not good; for some is certainly bad and some may be indifferent. And on the other hand, other things, besides conduct, may be good; and if they are so, then, 'good' denotes some property, that is common to them and conduct; and if we examine good conduct alone of all good things, then we shall be in danger of mistaking for this property, some property which is not shared by those other things . . . (Moore 1903, p. 54)

Thus good conduct is what has the two properties goodness and being conduct, goodness being the property that all good things have in common.

no difference from a moral point of view which she chooses. If, alternatively, one would be better than the other, then it is very plausible to think that morality requires her to choose that one: it could hardly be thought that morality declares in favor of the other, or even leaves it open for her to choose the other. So "Alice ought to give Bert a banana," for example, is true if and only if Alice's giving Bert a banana would be better than her not doing so. There are different theories about what marks one act as better than another; what matters for present purposes is only the idea that if we have an acceptable account of betterness for acts, then we have an acceptable account of the requirements of morality.

In short, as the third idea says, all of morality reduces ultimately to the properties goodness and badness and the relation betterness.

Now there is trouble, for the property goodness seems metaphysically mysterious. What could it come to for a thing to be good? For a thing to be good is presumably for it to be good that it exist; so presumably good things have a call on us to pursue their continued existence if they already exist, and their coming into existence if they do not. What a queer property, J. L. Mackie said. How could there be such a property in nature as to-be-pursuedness'![2] Moore's own response to this source of concern, namely "Ah well, goodness is a *non-natural* property, though of course a non-natural property that a thing possesses because of its natural properties" did not relieve the feeling of mystery. Similarly for the property badness: how could there be

---

[2] Mackie (1977), p. 40. Goodness (if there is such a property) has a kind of "magnetism", said Stevenson in Stevenson (1937, p. 13). It might be worth noticing that both Mackie and Stevenson had a weak form of magnetism in mind. As Mackie put it: "something's being good both tells the person who *knows* this to pursue it and makes him pursue it" (my italics). As Stevenson put it: "A person who *recognizes* X to be 'good' must ipso facto acquire a stronger tendency to act in its favor than he otherwise would have had" (my italics). That is weak. After all, an iron filing doesn't have to know or recognize that a thing is a magnet in order to be drawn to it. Aquinas appears to be attributing a stronger form of magnetism to goodness in saying "[a]ll things, not only those which have knowledge but also those which are without it, tend to good"; see Aquinas (1256–9), pp. 33–40. (I am indebted to Timothy Hinton for drawing my attention to those passages in Aquinas.)

such a property in nature as to-be-avoidedness! Similarly for the relation betterness: how could there be such a relation in nature as preferredness!

Given their metaphysical mysteriousness, these properties and this relation are epistemologically mysterious. If all morality reduces ultimately to these properties and this relation, finding out whether a moral sentence is true requires being able to find out which things possess them. But how is that to be done? What we observe on looking around us is the factual, the nonmoral; what mode of knowledge-gathering is to enable us to get from there to the conclusion that such and such things have or lack the (queer) properties goodness or badness, or the (queer) relation betterness? There seems to be no answer. The crack in the universe of discourse between the moral and the nonmoral seems to be too deep to be crossed in any way, and moral objectivity therefore seems to be a fantasy.

8.2 A number of philosophers have been saying in recent years that it is simply a mistake to believe that there is such a property as goodness.[3] What's wrong with goodness? When we look away from abstract discussions of the good – when we look at the things people regard as good, and why they do – what we see is a much more complicated phenomenon than philosophers such as Moore allowed for. People do say the words "That is good," but what they mean is always something more particular: what they mean is always that the thing in question is *good in a way*, a way that the context of utterance, or the speaker, has to supply on pain of our simply not knowing what he or she does mean. Perhaps the speaker means that the thing is a good hammer, or a good wine, or a good sunset. Or that the thing is good for his or her friends, or for the country, or for people at large, or for the living-room carpet. And so on, for indefinitely many other possibilities.

It seems very plausible to think that a thing's being good must consist in its being good in some way – thus that all goodness is goodness-in-a-way. If that is the case, then there is no meta-

---

[3] See Geach (1956), Ziff (1960), von Wright (1963), and Foot (1985). My own views (which will be briefly summarized in what follows) are in Thomson (1994).

physically mysterious property goodness, for being a good hammer isn't metaphysically mysterious, nor is being a good wine. A thing's possessing the only goodness a thing can possess, namely goodness-in-a-way, does not require that it possess, or even that there exist, a metaphysically queer property to-be-pursuedness: some people do pursue good hammers and good wines, but good hammers and good wines don't *call on* us to do so. In consequence, there is no general epistemological mystery about goodness. Finding out that a thing possesses the only goodness a thing can possess, namely goodness-in-a-way, does not require finding out that it possesses a metaphysically queer property to-be-pursuedness.

Similarly for badness: it is very plausible to think that a thing's being bad must consist in its being bad in some way — thus that all badness is badness-in-a-way.

Accepting that all goodness is goodness-in-a-way and all badness badness-in-a-way results in a demystification of goodness and badness. It also results in a demystification of betterness. Alice's new Mercedes is a good car; chocolate tastes good. Which is better, Alice's Mercedes or chocolate? It's a crazy question. One is good in one way, the other in another, and all goodness being goodness-in-a-way, so also is all betterness betterness-in-a-way.

Demystifying goodness, badness, and betterness leaves questions, of course. We are left with the metaphysical question what it is for a thing to be good in this way or that; and answering that question is a precondition for answering the further question whether it is possible to find out that a thing is good in this or that way, and if so how. But the question "What is it for a hammer to be a good one?" is less baffling than the question "What is it for a thing to be (pure, unadulterated) *good*?" (It is a matter of interest, which should have been taken more seriously, that in order to get students to worry about this latter question we have first to talk them into believing that there is such a question.[4]) And we are markedly less tempted to think it impossible to find out that a thing is a good hammer

---

[4] We should have taken more seriously the weirdness of the passage early in Moore (1903) — p. 55 — that aims to make clear to us what question he is going to be asking in asking "What is good?" He says: " 'Books are good' would be an

than we are to think it impossible to find out that a thing is (pure, unadulterated) good. Global sceptics apart, we all believe that we do find out such facts as that one hammer is a good one and another a bad one, and such facts as that a Mercedes is a better car than a Buick, and indeed, that we find them out every day. In short, the project of trying to understand the metaphysics and epistemology of goodness seems less hopeless after demystification.

I don't for a moment deny that some ways of being good are puzzling in ways that others are not; but that is not because they are ways of being good, it is rather because of the ways of being good that they are.

On the other hand, the question what it comes to for morality to require that we do a thing, and therefore how we find such things out, may now appear markedly harder than it originally did. The point here might be put in this way: demystifying goodness, badness, and betterness seems to mystify moral requirement. On the assumption that there is such a relation as betterness, it seemed to be easy to say what moral requirement consists in. Given that there is such a relation as betterness, it follows that whenever a person, say Alice, is confronted with a choice between doing alpha or not doing alpha, either her doing alpha would be better than her not doing alpha, or her not doing alpha would be better than her doing alpha, or neither would be better than the other. And it seemed right to conclude that "Morality requires Alice to give Bert a banana," for example, is true if and only if Alice's giving Bert a banana would be better than her not doing so. If there is no such relation as betterness, what *are* the truth conditions of "Morality requires Alice to give Bert a banana"?

Let us distinguish between two kinds of sentence. I will call the first *evaluatives*. These are sentences by the assertion of which we predicate goodness in a way, or badness in a way, or

---

answer to it, . . ." Books are good? Books are good *whats*?! Moore goes on: "though an answer obviously false; for some books are very bad indeed. And ethical judgments of this kind do indeed belong to Ethics; etc. etc." Well, some books are bad books. Some books are bad for children to read. What sense could be made of a person who said "No, no, I meant that some books are pure, unadulterated *bad things*"?

betterness in a way. The second are *directives*: these are senten-ces by the assertion of which we predicate of a person that he or she ought or should or must or is morally required, or is under a duty or obligation, to do or to refrain from doing, a thing.[5]

And let us begin with the evaluatives. For the most part, I will attend only to those by the assertion of which we predicate goodness in a way.

8.3 The ways of being good form a large clutter, and there are a variety of ways of dividing them up. One intuitively attractive way is to divide them into sub-classes as follows. (My way of dividing the territory comes, with modifications, from von Wright (1963).)

Some things are good for use in doing a thing. For example, a certain hammer might be good for use in hammering in nails, a certain fountain pen might be good for use in writing, a certain knife might be good for use in carving. Being good for use in hammering in nails, being good for use in writing, being good for use in carving are ways of being good; the sub-class of the ways of being good that they fall into may be called the *useful*.

Some people are good at doing this or that: thus Alice might be good at hanging wallpaper, Bert might be good at singing, Carol might be good at playing chess. Being good at hanging wallpaper, being good at singing, being good at playing chess are ways of being good; this sub-class may be called the *skillful*.

Some things are good to look at or listen to and so on. A certain sunset might be good to look at. A certain wine might taste good. A certain novel might be good to read. Being good to look at, being good-tasting, being good to read are ways of being good; this sub-class may be called the *enjoyable*.

Some things are good for something. Drinking lemonade might be good for Smith, who has a cold. An increase in fund-ing for public education might be good for children and thereby for the country as a whole. Weekly vacuuming might be good for the living-room carpet. Being good for Smith, being good for

---

[5] David Wiggins called these sentences "evaluations" and "directives" in Wig-gins (1976) p. 95.

children, being good for the living-room carpet are ways of being good; this sub-class may be called the *beneficial*.

Finally, some things are morally good in one or another way. A certain act or kind of act or person might be morally good, or, more particularly, just or generous or brave or tactful or considerate and so on. This sub-class of the ways of being good may be called the *morally good*.

In sum, here are five sub-classes of the class of ways of being good: the useful, skillful, enjoyable, beneficial, and morally good. Two points are worth drawing attention to before we move on.

In the first place, the sub-classes interconnect. Thus Bert is good in a way if he is good at singing (skillful); but Bert is good at singing only if his singing is good to listen to (enjoyable). A certain fountain pen is good in a way if it is good for use in writing (useful); but it is good for use in writing only if the product of writing with it looks good (enjoyable).

Second, some people have been overly fascinated by the fact that a thing can be good for one person and not for another, as, for example, drinking lemonade might be good for Smith, who has a cold, but not good for Jones, who has an ulcer. I say "overly fascinated" since they have concluded from the existence of such cases that goodness is relative. Now there may be reason to regard goodness as in one or another way relative to something; we will return to this idea in section 8.5 below. But it pays to stress that goodness is not everywhere relative in the way in which the beneficial is relative. The beneficial is of course, and by definition, relative in the following way: a thing that is *good for* something is good *for something*. But the beneficial does not exhaust the ways of being good. Suppose we tell a person that Carol is good at playing chess, or that such and such a wine tastes good, and our hearer asks "For whom?" This question has no answer, nor does it need one.

Do all of the ways of being good fall into one or other of the five sub-classes I have drawn attention to?[6] I should think not. But if we had an intuitively plausible account of these ways of

---

[6] It is perhaps worth mention that for many kinds K, being a good K is analyzable into being a K that is good in a way falling into one of our five sub-classes. Thus being a good hammer is presumably being a hammer that is

being good, we would have ground for hope that something like it would work for the remaining ways.

8.4 What makes a thing be good? Intuitively, the goodness of a thing must issue in some way or other from its *answering to wants*. (That it must is an intuition with a long history.[7]) So in particular for the ways of being good: a thing's being good in this or that way must issue from its answering to wants. That is plausibly viewable as what all of the ways of being good have in common, namely that a thing's being good in each way issues from its answering to wants – its answering to wants in the relevant way, of course, for a thing's being good in way W might well be expected to issue from its answering to wants in a different way from the way in which a thing's being good in way W' does.

So it would be very welcome if we could produce an account, for each of the ways of being good, of how a thing's being good in that way issues from the thing's answering to wants. If we could produce such an account, we would have gone beyond demystifying goodness to naturalizing it, and indeed, to naturalizing it in an attractively stark way.

What follows, then, is a brief and very rough sketch of such an account, at all events for the ways of being good that I have drawn attention to. My suggestions are merely suggestions, and they contain no novelties; what I mainly do is to bring together a number of more or less familiar considerations from different areas – I think it a good idea to look at them together. Since I am in doubt as to whether such an account *can* be produced, I will point along the way to some of the more serious difficulties that producing such an account would require one to overcome. If

---

good for use in hammering in nails. Being a good wallpaper hanger is presumably being a wallpaper hanger who is good at hanging wallpaper. And so on. Indeed, I think that the role of "good" as modifier on a kind-term (as in expressions of the form "good K") is parasitic on the role of "good" modified (as in expressions of the form "good for use in," "good at," "good for," and so on). For discussion, see Thomson (1994).

[7] An interesting recent effort to give flesh to this intuition is by David Lewis: see Lewis (1989) and Johnston (1989). Lewis's theory is a theory about how a thing's possessing the (as I think it, pseudo-) property goodness issues from the thing's answering to wants.

any are not merely serious but fatal, then that fact would itself be of great interest in that it would show there is something deeply wrong with the intuition that a thing's goodness issues from its answering to wants.

8.5 Let us begin with the sub-class of the useful. It includes being good for use in hammering in nails. What is it for a thing to be good for use in hammering in nails? The short answer is: being such as to facilitate hammering nails in *well*.

But what is hammering nails in well? Here is a sugestion: a person, say Alice, is hammering nails in well if and only if she is hammering them in in a manner such that her hammering them in in that manner conduces to her satisfying the want she is hammering them in to satisfy. Thus suppose she is hammering nails in as part of the process of building a bookcase. Hammering the nails in straight, firmly, without denting the surface into which they are being hammered, and so on, would presumably conduce to her succeeding in building the bookcase, and if so, she is hammering the nails in well if that is the manner in which she is hammering them in. Different wants might call for hammering nails in in a different manner. (Perhaps for some purposes, hammering nails in crookedly is required.) What matters is only that Alice's manner of hammering the nails in conduces to her satisfying her want, whatever it may be.

This suggestion won't do as it stands, but I think that something like it must be right.[8]

Now I doubt that a thing's being good for use in hammering in nails requires its being such as to facilitate hammering them in in manners that conduce to satisfying all of the wants that anyone on any occasion is hammering nails in to satisfy. What matters is the wants people typically hammer nails in to satisfy. Building bookshelves, for example, or houses. Or hanging pictures. And so on. So I think that something like the following must be right:

---

[8] For example, perverse wants need to be ruled out. A teacher of carpentry might hammer some nails in badly, in order to demonstrate hammering nails in badly. His hammering them in is not marked as hammering them in well – by hypothesis, he is hammering them in badly – by virtue of the fact that his hammering them in in that manner conduces to his satisfying the want he is hammering them in to satisfy.

Usefulness Example: being good for use in hammering in nails consists in being such as to facilitate hammering nails in in manners that conduce to satisfying the wants people typically hammer nails in to satisfy.

More generally:

Usefulness Generalization: being good for use in X-ing consists in being such as to facilitate X-ing in manners that conduce to satisfying the wants people typically X to satisfy.

We need to be clear about what theses obtainable from this generalization identify being good for use in X-ing *with*. The Usefulness Example identifies being good for use in hammering in nails with

being such as to facilitate hammering nails in in manners that conduce to satisfying the wants people typically hammer nails in to satisfy.

Which things meet this condition? Given the wants people typically hammer nails in to satisfy, a thing meets it only if it is well balanced, strong, with an easily graspable handle, and so on. But the Usefulness Example does not identify being good for use in hammering in nails with

being well balanced, strong, with an easily graspable handle, and so on.

And that, I suggest, is as it should be. There are a lot of very odd possible worlds, and I am sure there are some in which the wants people typically hammer nails in to satisfy are very different. Perhaps in a given world people don't make houses or bookshelves with nails: perhaps they hammer nails in only for decorative purposes, and perhaps what conduces to satisfying their wants is something whose use produces lots of bent nails, split wood, denting, and all round splatter. We may suppose that large slabs of granite facilitate hammering nails in in that manner. I think we should grant that large slabs of granite are good for use in hammering in nails in that world.

This could be denied. That is, we could insist that the people in that world hammer nails in for the wrong reasons, and that large slabs of granite are not in any world good for use in hammering in nails. But that seems to me an odd form of metaphysical imperialism. Why should it be *our* wants that fix what marks a thing as good for use in hammering in nails in every possible world?

If we are not metaphysical imperialists, we will allow that large slabs of granite are good for use in hammering in nails in their world. And we can say so compatibly with accepting the Usefulness Example, since that thesis identifies being good for use in hammering in nails, not with being well balanced, strong, with an easily graspable handle, and so on, but only with facilitating hammering nails in in manners that conduce to satisfying typical wants, and by hypothesis, large slabs of granite do so in their world – just as well balanced hammers do so in ours.

To take this line is to reject yet another thesis that comes down to us from G. E. Moore. Moore said that goodness 'strongly supervenes' on a thing's 'intrinsic nature'. (The term "strong supervenience" did not occur in Moore, but the idea did.) What Moore had in mind was (roughly) this: it cannot be the case that a thing X is good and a thing Y is not good though X and Y have the same nonrelational properties. Alternatively put: if a thing X in our world is good, then anything in any other possible world that shares X's nonrelational properties is also good. Or again: if a thing X in our world is not good, then anything in any other possible world that shares X's nonrelational properties is also not good. Now what Moore was talking about was (pure, unadulterated) goodness, not goodness-in-a-way; and he might very well not have said this about the ways of being good I have been pointing to. In any case, the line I here recommend rejects that idea. For I here recommend allowing that a thing X in our world (for example, a large slab of granite) is not in fact good for use in hammering in nails, though a thing in another possible world that shares X's non-relational properties is in that world good for use in hammering in nails.

Indeed, the intuition we are looking at says that all of the ways of being good – not just being good for use in hammering in nails, not just being good in any of the ways falling into the sub-class of the useful – are relative in this sense: whether a thing is good in a way turns on whether it answers to wants. But what is wanted in one world differs from what is wanted in another. So if the intuition we are looking at is right, then, while it can be said that goodness supervenes in Moore's sense on wants, goodness does not supervene in that sense on the nonrelational properties of the things that possess it.

8.6 Let us turn to the other sub-classes of ways of being good. The skillful is easy to deal with if we were right about the useful. What is it to be good at hanging wallpaper? The short answer is: being capable of hanging wallpaper *well*.

What is hanging wallpaper well? Here is a suggestion: a person, say Alice, is hanging wallpaper well if and only if she is hanging it in the manner that people who want to hang wallpaper typically want to hang it in. What manner is that? Securely, without bubbles, with no spaces between the sheets, and so on. But that's only this world; in a different world, people might delight in wallpaper bubbles. So let us identify being good at hanging wallpaper, not with being capable of hanging it securely, without bubbles, with no spaces between the sheets, and so on, but instead with being capable of hanging it in the manner (whatever it may be) that people who want to hang wallpaper typically want to hang it in.

More generally:

Skillfulness Generalization:	being good at X-ing consists in being capable of X-ing in the manner that people who want to X typically want to X in.

8.7 A much harder problem is presented by the sub-class of the enjoyable. This sub-class includes being good to look at or listen to, it includes tasting good, being good to read, and so on and on.

What is being good to look at? We might start in this way: a thing's being good to look at consists in its being such as to please or satisfy people by its looks. But this won't do. Kitsch pleases a lot of people by its looks, yet is not really good to look at. (After all, it is goodness we are concerned with, not mere likes and dislikes.)

Similarly for tasting good. We can't say that a thing's tasting good consists in its being such as to please people by its taste, for there is kitsch in food and drink too, and it too is popular. (Koolaid may not please *you*, but it sells remarkably well.)

So it looks as if we need to impose a constraint. But what constraint?

A familiar move is to constrain the people who matter for these purposes to experts, or competent critics, or "true judges."[9] A person might be an expert when it comes to paintings, but not when it comes to gardens; and a person might be an expert when it comes to soft drinks, but not when it comes to wines. So the idea would presumably go like this: a K's being good to look at consists in its being such as to please, by its looks, those who are experts in Ks, and a K's tasting good consists in its being such as to please, by its taste, those who are experts in Ks, and so on.

But that familiar move presents a familiar and very hard problem. For who are the experts? What marks Alice as an expert in paintings, and Bert as an expert in wines? It won't do to explain that a person's being an expert in paintings consists in his or her being pleased by and only by paintings that are good to look at if we hope to be saying something informative in going on to say that a painting's being good to look at consists in its pleasing those who are experts in paintings.

Something like the following is obviously the way to begin on the matter. Experts in Ks have had a broad acquaintance with

---

[9] "True judge" is Hume's phrase; see Hume (1757). Arguably, a similar constraint needs to be imposed in the sub-classes of the useful and skillful.

Ks: experts in paintings have looked at a lot of different kinds of paintings, and experts in wines have tasted a lot of different kinds of wines. This broader acquaintance has issued in their being able to make distinctions among Ks, and therefore in their noticing more in Ks than the rest of us do – the expert in paintings sees more in a painting than I do, the expert in wines tastes more in a wine than I do. (Of course, the more that the expert sees or tastes had better be there to be seen or tasted.[10]) Consensus matters too: wildly discordant judgments may be right, but their being wildly discordant means that there is reason to think they are not. And so does convergence over time matter: Smith may be thought an expert at one time and at a later time, perhaps in a later generation, turn out not to have been. (The availability of an explanation of Smith's mistakes is crucial if we are to be justified in calling them *mistakes.*) But these considerations are merely where one begins.

We should keep in mind, however, that it really isn't in question whether there is such a thing as being an expert in paintings or wines; nor is it really in question what in broad outline does or does not lend weight to the conclusion that this is true of a person. The philosopher's very hard problem is what exactly makes this true of a person, but the fact that that

---

[10] Sometimes it is. Here is Hume, retelling a story from *Don Quixote*: "It is with good reason, says SANCHO to the squire with the great nose, that I pretend to have a judgment in wine. This is a quality hereditary in our family. Two of my kinsmen were once called to give their opinion of a hogshead, which was supposed to be excellent, being old and of a good vintage. One of them tastes it; considers it; and after mature reflection pronounces the wine to be good, were it not for a small taste of leather, which he perceived in it. The other, after using the same precautions, gives also his verdict in favor of the wine; but with the reserve of a taste of iron, which he could easily distinguish. You cannot imagine how much they were both ridiculed for their judgment. But who laughed in the end? On emptying the hogshead, there was found at the bottom, an old key with a leathern thong tied to it." (Hume 1757, p. 272).

Mary Mothersill suggests that "confirmation of the kinsmen's judgment requires not that the hogshead be emptied but that less articulate wine-tasters should say (on the second try) 'Exactly right! A slightly leathery, slightly metallic aftertaste.'" (Mothersill, 1984, p. 195. See also her discussion of Hume's essay in Mothersill, 1989.) It would be even more helpful if they explicitly added " . . . and a leathery, metallic aftertaste is unpleasant in a wine."

problem is hard is compatible with its being a fact that some people are experts.

In any case, the intuition we are looking at says that being a painting that is good to look at, or a wine that tastes good, *consists in* being such as to please. Thus we are not to think of the experts as better detectors than thee or me of evaluative properties that transcend the fact of a thing's being such as to give pleasure, the thing's being such as to give pleasure being merely a sign of the possession of the evaluative property: possession of the evaluative property by a thing just is the thing's being such as to give pleasure. In short, the intuition we are looking at says that being a painting that is good to look at, and so on, is no more transcendent a property than being good to use for hammering in nails and being good at hanging wallpaper. That, anyway, seems to me to be very plausible.

But it will have been noticed that this account of the enjoyable – unlike the account of the useful and the skillful in the preceding sections – naturalizes the enjoyable in terms of pleasure or satisfaction, not wants. Is pleasure reducible in some way to wants? Or alternatively, are wants reducible in some way to pleasure? We have a unified naturalization of the ways of being good only if reduction in one or other direction is possible. There must surely be a close connection between what pleases a person and what he or she wants, but I am going to have to leave this open.

8.8 Let us turn now to the still more complex, and for our purposes more important, sub-class of the beneficial. I mentioned in section 8.2 that something might be good for a person, a country, or a carpet. So also might a thing be good for a tree or a cat or a person's throat. What is it for a thing X to be good for a thing Y? X's being good for Y presumably consists in X's being conducive to Y's welfare, or to Y's being in good condition, or anyway to Y's being in better condition than it would otherwise be.

But what does Y's being in good condition consist in? The answer surely varies with the kind or kinds Y falls into. I will be able to discuss only a few of them, and only very briefly at that. My main aim will be to bring out some differences, some of which make serious – arguably fatal – trouble for the intuition we are looking at.

Carpets are an easy case. I should think that a carpet's being in good condition consists in something like this: its being in the condition C such that people who want a carpet typically want a carpet in that condition. In this world, people who want a carpet typically want a carpet that will last a long time, and look good while it lasts; so if we want a carpet, we typically want a carpet that is in the following condition C: has no ground in dirt, is unstained, is not flattened or frayed or threadbare, and so on. No doubt the wanted condition is different in other possible worlds.

Analogously for lawn mowers, and many other kinds of physical objects, manufactured or not.

Living creatures are another matter, however, and in the case of some kinds, much harder to square with the intuition.

Consider plants. A carpet's being in good condition consists in its being in the condition C that answers to wants; can we say that a plant's being in good condition consists in its being in the condition C that answers to wants? Alas for the intuition, we don't seem to be able to.

For it is very plausible to think (i) that a plant's being in good condition consists in its being in the following condition C: healthy. And (ii) that what makes it the case that a plant is healthy has nothing to do with anybody's wants: the question whether a plant is healthy is not to be answered by finding out what people want in plants, but rather by finding out features of the species the plant is a member of.[11] And (iii) that what makes it the case that health is the relevant condition C also has nothing to do with anybody's wants.

Some examples will help. (i) An apple tree is in good condition just in case it is in the following condition C: healthy. (ii) What makes it the case that an apple tree is healthy is its having the features normal for its species. And (iii) what makes it the

---

[11] There are a number of quite general characterizations of health in the literature of bio-medical ethics. Here is Norman Daniels': "health is the absence of disease, and diseases (I include deformities and disabilities that result from trauma) are deviations from the natural functional organization of a typical member of a species" (Daniels, 1985, p. 28. I have omitted his italics.)

case that health is the relevant condition C – that is, what makes it the case that a healthy apple tree *is* an apple tree in good condition – also has nothing to do with anybody's wants. No doubt an apple tree that is healthy is in the condition such that people who want an apple tree typically want one in that condition, for healthy apple trees are likely to supply more and better fruit, and to live longer and look better while they live, than they would if they were not healthy, and these are things we want in an apple tree when we want an apple tree. But it isn't our wanting a healthy apple tree when we want an apple tree that makes health be the relevant condition C.

Point (iii) emerges starkly when we turn to a second example. Kudzu vines are aggressive and invasive and, when healthy, almost impossible to get rid of or even to control. Hardly anybody wants them. Those who do, however, want stunted, weakened ones: just sturdy enough for use to prevent erosion, but sufficiently weak to be controllable.[12] Nevertheless it is a healthy kudzu vine that is in good condition, not one that is unhealthy.

And then there are the plants that nobody wants at all. A recent article in *The New York Times* (August 16, 1994, p. C4) reports the appearance in the upper South of a new species of vine, which "might be called Son of Kudzu, a nasty and equally aggressive invader from abroad with no apparent redeeming economic or social value". Nobody wants a Son of Kudzu. Still, a Son of Kudzu is in good condition just in case it is healthy.

I have mentioned only plants by way of troublemakers, but similar points presumably hold for at least some animals as well. Other things being equal, a cat that has been declawed is in worse condition than one that has not, despite the fact that our wants might be better answered to by declawing it.

Can the intuition we are looking at be preserved in face of these considerations? I can't see how. Two further considerations are worth drawing attention to, however. In the first place, it should puzzle us that a plant's being in good condition should be an exception to an intuition that works so well for

---

[12] I am indebted to Catherine Elgin for this information about kudzu vines and those who want them.

other ways of being good. Notice in particular that a good apple tree just is one that answers to contextually relevant wants, and so also for a good kudzu vine (and a good cat); a good Son of Kudzu would be one that answered to wants, and that none do means that none are good – to borrow a bad joke, the only good Son of Kudzu is a dead one. What makes trouble in the case of those kinds is not what makes an instance good of its kind but only what makes its condition good. That is puzzling. Second, while it seems undeniable that what marks a plant as in good condition is its being healthy, the question is worth asking just what is supposed to be *good* about a plant's being healthy if we are not allowed to mention answering to wants in our answer? A healthy plant is a plant that is likely to live longer, and reproduce more profusely, than it otherwise would; but what's good about its doing so if we don't care whether it does, or even positively want it not to? I will unfortunately have to bypass these matters.

I have suggested that plants (and some animals) make trouble for the intuition; what about people? I think they do not. Health is certainly a factor in a person's being in good condition, but we can answer the question what's good about a person's being healthy, and wants are at the heart of the answer: healthy people are able to do more of the things that people typically want to do than they would be if they were not healthy.

But health is neither sufficient nor necessary for a person's being in good condition. It is not sufficient, since a person can be healthy and all the same miserable. It is also not necessary. Most of us do want to be healthy, but some (perhaps many) of us are prepared to trade off at least *a* measure of health for the sake of other things. The great saint, the great physicist, the great chess-player, might have had to sacrifice a substantial measure of health in order to succeed in his or her chosen life. That is compatible with their lives' being deeply satisfying, and their condition therefore good.

I mentioned the great chess-player as well as the great saint and the great physicist in order to stress that it is not the value of the activity, or of its fruits, that marks these people as in good condition. Chess not only produces nothing, it is merely a game, with no further significance; yet one can find fulfillment in it.

It emerges, then, that what is crucial to a person's well-being is what that particular, individual person wants. Not what others want of or for the person. (Contrast carpets.) Not what is typically wanted. A person's well-being consists in his or her own life's going as he or she wants it to.

More precisely, a person's well-being consists in his or her life's going as he or she wants it to subject to constraints of two kinds. On the one hand, the life the person is leading has to have been chosen in awareness of its costs, including opportunity costs. On the other hand, the choice has to have been autonomously made – that is, in the absence of such improper 'preference-bendings' as issue from threats, or drugs, or a grossly unjust political regime. But we can accommodate these two constraints by appeal to wants: people do not merely want their lives to go in this way rather than that, they also have second-order wants about the etiology of the first-order wants that are going to issue in their decisions about how to live.

But I fancy that these constraints are less strict than they are sometimes said to be. If a person's life is going as he or she wants it to be going, and the person has no regrets and will continue to have no regrets, and if, moreover, his or her choices were made in light of a measure of awareness of the costs, and in a measure autonomously, then that seems to be enough. For it should be remembered that a person's condition may be good compatibly with its being the case that it could have been better.

8.9 Let us turn now to moral goodness. Just as there is no (pure, unadulterated) goodness, so also is there no (pure, unadulterated) moral goodness. Everything that is good is good-in-a-way; so also is everything that is morally good morally-good-in-a-way – generous, or brave, or just, or considerate, and so on.

It might be worth drawing attention to the fact that I do not include being good for a person, or for people, among the ways of being morally good. An act may be good for all those affected by it; that leaves entirely open whether it is morally good – to find out whether the act is morally good we need to find out whether it is generous or brave or just and so on. Similarly for a state of affairs that consists in a person's getting what is good for him or her, or a state of affairs that consists in a person's being in good condition: while states of affairs presumably can't be generous, or brave, and so on, they can be just, and these had better be if they are to be morally good.

And now: what have the ways of being morally good got to do with our wants? Moral goodness connects with wants by way of connecting with other, nonmoral ways of being good. The ways of being morally good are second order: they rest on the ways of being good that we have already surveyed.

Other things besides acts and states of affairs can be morally good: people, distributions, political systems, and so on. I will have space only for very sketchy remarks about generosity, bravery, and justice in action.

Generosity in action has what might be called an intensional connection with the beneficial – and thereby with wants – since an act is generous only if its agent believes that it is good for someone. You don't have actually to succeed in doing what is good for someone; you do have to believe you are doing this.

Generosity in action also has a less direct connection with the beneficial by virtue of the further conditions an act must meet if it is to be generous. You have to believe, not merely that your act is good for someone, you have to believe that it is good for someone other than yourself, that it is in a measure costly, and indeed, costly to you yourself, and that it is not required by justice. (However good it may be for my grocer that I pay his bill, and however costly to me, my paying his bill is not a generous act. Not because my act is mean or ungenerous, rather because it is neither.) The less direct connection with the beneficial then emerges in this way. Suppose Alice acted out of these beliefs. Even if one or more of them were false, still, her acting generously is a good sign that she is a generous person, that is, that she is disposed to do what she believes is good for others, at a measure of cost to herself, even where justice does not require her to do so. That there are people so disposed in our community is good for us generally.

Bravery in action too has an intensional connection with other ways of being good, since an act is brave only if its agent believes that it is, or that its outcome will be, good in some way.

But the intensional object of a given brave act need not be the beneficial. (For example, its intensional object might instead be justice.)

And bravery in action also has a similar, less direct connection with the beneficial. Suppose Alice acted out of the belief that she would be doing something good in a way, and that she was incurring a risk in doing so. Then she acted bravely. Even if her beliefs were false, her acting bravely is a good sign that she is a brave person, that is, that she is disposed to do what she believes is good in a way, at a risk to herself. That there are people so disposed in our community is good for us generally.

Justice in action is harder to give even a quick sketch of, partly (though only partly) because of our tendency to spread it across the entire moral terrain: we are tempted to think of all morally good acts as just and all morally bad ones unjust. It is not obvious why we are tempted to do this. In any case, to yield to this temptation is to lose sight of something that is specially involved in justice in action under a narrower construal of it, a something that is not involved in generosity or bravery.

What I have in mind is a construal of justice in action according to which a person's act, say Alice's, was just only if she believed her act was the according to a person of what she *owed* the person – of what was *due to* the person from her. The promisor owes it to the promisee to do what he or she promised. The person who volunteers to speak owes it to his or her hearers to not lie to them. I owe it to my grocer to pay his bill. I owe it to you to not cut down your tree or kick your shin without your permission. And so on. By contrast, we are not in general owed what is good for us or what is good in any other way. If Alice saves me or my house, she may act generously or bravely; other things being equal, she does not owe it to me to do what she does, and thus does not act justly. Not because she acts unjustly. Rather her act is neither.[13]

Now this notion due to or owed to obviously calls for analysis, and it is disputable (and disputed) how it should be analyzed. I

---

[13] Is it because we think "just" and "unjust" are exhaustive of the possibilities that we are tempted to spread justice across the entire moral terrain? For if they did exhaust the possibilities – if it could not be the case that an act was neither

will not go into the matter any further here. It is perhaps worth stress, however, given our purposes, that whatever exactly it may come to for me to owe it to you to pay you five dollars today, we can all of us imagine finding out that I do – as, for example, by finding out that you very kindly loaned me five dollars on my promise to repay you today. Finding such things out is no more abstruse or arcane a matter than finding out that a person would be acting generously or bravely in doing this or that.

I suggest that we adopt this narrow construal of justice in action. How does it, so construed, connect with wants? Generosity and bravery in action have what I called an intensional connection with ways of being good; not so justice in action. But justice in action has a similar less direct connection with the beneficial. Alice's acting justly is a good sign that she is a just person, that is, that she is disposed to do what she believes she owes to others; and that there are people so disposed in our community is good for us generally – indeed, it is hard to see how we could so much as *be* a community unless a substantial number of us were so disposed.

What may well be asked, however, is why these ways of being good are singled out and thought of as ways of being *morally* good. That is because of their connection with the directives, to which we should now turn.

8.10 The directives, I said, are sentences by the assertion of which we predicate of a person that he or she ought or should or must or is morally required, or is under a duty or obligation, to do or to refrain from doing, a thing. Let us give the name Moral-Requirement-Sentences to sentences of the form "Morality requires X to do (or: to not do) alpha".

---

just nor unjust – then it is plain enough that all good acts would be just, since no good act is unjust.

A second possible source of the temptation I describe may be the very fact that an acceptable account of the notion 'owed to' at work here is so hard to come by. My remarks in the text are over-simple. What is in question here are rights, and indeed, rights that are not 'overridden'. The literature on this topic is immense; my own views may be found in Thomson (1990).

I suggest that Moral-Requirement-Sentences are fundamental to the directives in the following way: no directive is true if morality requires the subject to not do the thing in question. Thus consider

(1)   Alice ought to eat a banana.

(1), I should think, is false if morality requires Alice to not eat a banana.

Is that suggestion correct? One argument to the effect that it is not issues from a fairly widely held view to the effect that the word "ought" is ambiguous, and indeed, that directives such as (1) have (at least) the following two meanings. One meaning (it is said) is

(1_C)   Morality requires Alice to eat a banana.

It is common to say that (1), so interpreted, is a categorical imperative, "categorical" in that the truth-value of (1_C)– and thus the truth-value of (1), so interpreted – does not turn on what Alice wants. So interpreted, (1) is of course false if morality requires Alice to not eat a banana, for (1_C) is false if morality requires Alice to not eat a banana.

A second meaning of (1) (it is said) is

(1_H)   Alice's wants would most efficiently be answered to by her eating a banana.

It is common to say that (1), so interpreted, is a hypothetical imperative, "hypothetical" in that the truth-value of (1_H) – and thus the truth-value of (1), so interpreted – does turn on what Alice wants. So interpreted, (1) can be true compatibly with its being the case that morality requires Alice to not eat a banana. And my suggestion that moral-requirement sentences are fundamental is therefore not true of directives such as (1) so interpreted.

Now this seems to me to be a mistake. Suppose Bert is trying to take Alice's eyes out: he really does want to do this. He is not doing the job efficiently, however, since he is using a wooden spoon. And now consider the sentence

(2) Bert ought to use a knife.

It would indeed most efficiently answer to Bert's wants to use a knife, so

(2_H) Bert's wants would most efficiently be answered to by his using a knife

is true. But (2) does not have (2_H) among its meanings: (2) has no meaning at all under which it is true – (2) is just plain false. (Whatever Bert's wants may be, what is true is rather that he ought not use a knife. He ought not use a wooden spoon either. What he ought to do is to stop trying to take Alice's eyes out.) So (2) has no meaning under which it is a hypothetical imperative.

It is at least as clear that (2) does not mean

(2_C) Morality requires Bert to use a knife.

Suppose Alice and I are watching Bert, who is trying to eat his steak with a fork. I say to Alice: "Bert ought to use a knife." That is not made false by the fact (we can suppose it a fact) that morality does not require Bert to use a knife.

Perhaps though (2) does not mean (2_C) it nevertheless has (2_C) among its meanings? I see no good reason to think it does. There are plenty of bad reasons to think that (2) has (2_C) among its meanings. Here is an example: the fact that we often say "Bert ought to do alpha" because we think morality requires Bert to do alpha. The fact that we often say "Bert ought to do alpha" because we think morality requires Bert to do alpha is a bad reason for thinking that "Bert ought to do alpha" has "Morality requires Bert to do alpha" among its meanings. We often say "Somebody did alpha" because we think Bert did; that is a bad reason for thinking that "Somebody did alpha" has "Bert did alpha" among its meanings. I know of no better reason than this one.

In sum, (2) has no meaning under which it is a hypothetical imperative and has no meaning under which it is a categorical imperative. And so also for (1) and any other sentence of the form "X ought to do alpha".

What *does* "ought" mean, then? That seems to me a harder question than it is usually taken to be. It seems to me that an answer to it has to be such as to accommodate the following three principles. "X ought to do alpha" is false if morality requires X to not do alpha. "X ought to do alpha" is true if morality requires X to do alpha. And if morality neither requires X to do alpha nor requires X to not do alpha, then "X ought to do alpha" is true only if X has wants (or interests?) that will be answered to by his doing alpha.[14] (Thus wants are relevant only in the space not already occupied by moral requirements.) I have to bypass the question what account of the meaning of "ought" accommodates these principles.

I suggested that Moral-Requirement-Sentences are fundamental to the directives in the following way: no directive is true if morality requires the subject to not do the thing in question. Let us in any case now focus on them.

8.11 Under what conditions is a Moral-Requirement-Sentence true? Intuitively, what morality requires of us is what it would be morally bad for us to fail to do. So I suggest that we should take seriously the following idea:

---

[14] Some of us engage in a bit of fraud when we introduce our beginning students to the distinction between hypothetical and categorical imperatives. We tell them that

(3) Alice ought to put anti-freeze in her car

is a hypothetical imperative, in that – as we invite them to agree – (3) is false if there is nothing that Alice wants that she would get by putting anti-freeze in her car. Then we tell them that

(4) Bert ought to refrain from beating his children

is a categorical imperative, in that – as we invite them to agree – (4) is true even if there is nothing that Bert wants that he would get by refraining from beating his children. But this difference between (3) and (4) is not a difference between what is said by (3) and (4), or between what we say in saying them; it is entirely due to the background fact (which we are trading on our students' assuming) that morality requires Bert to refrain from beating his children and does not require Alice to put anti-freeze in her car.

Thesis of Moral-Requirement: a person is morally required to do a thing just in case his or her refraining from doing the thing would be morally bad in some way – mean or cowardly or unjust and so on.[15]

It would no doubt be good in a variety of ways if we did more than merely avoid meanness, cowardice, injustice, and so on; but intuitively, what morality *requires* of us is merely what any decent person is expected to do. It should be kept in mind, however, that that "merely" is not a sign that decency is always easy. Mere decency may require a good bit of a person, and it does if he is particularly unfortunate in his circumstances. In some circumstances, acting decently deserves as much praise as (perhaps even more praise than) acting more than decently does in more fortunate circumstances.

It is in this way that the ways of being morally good are marked as ways of being *morally* good: morality requires avoiding their contraries.

The Thesis of Moral-Requirement faces a number of difficulties, of which the following seems to me the most interesting. Suppose

(1)   Alice's refraining from doing alpha would be unjust

is true. Then the thesis yields that morality requires Alice to do alpha. Could it be the case that

(2)   Alice's doing alpha would be cowardly

[15] This thesis relativizes moral requirement to a person's beliefs, since moral badness in action, like moral goodness in action, is a function of the agent's beliefs. Thus consider a man who is so far benighted as to not know that he owes it to his grocer to pay his grocery bill. Then his refraining from paying the bill is not unjust. We may suppose also that it is not mean or cowardly. The thesis yields, then, that he is not morally required to pay his grocery bill. If you suppose (as I do) that that is unacceptable – if you suppose that the requirements of morality can in general be unwittingly met or breached – you will insist on a revision of the thesis to incorporate some such qualification as I have italicized in the following: a person X is morally required to do a thing just in case *if X knew what refraining from doing the thing would involve*, then X's refraining from doing the thing would be morally bad in some way – unjust or cowardly or mean and so on. For simplicity, I ignore this qualification in the text above.

is also true? Suppose it could. Suppose, then, that (2) is true. Then the thesis yields that morality requires Alice to not do alpha. What follows is that morality requires her both to do alpha and also to not do alpha. Is *that* a possibility?

On some views, it is entirely possible for morality to require a person to do alpha and to not do alpha. Friends of those views would agree that a person so situated is in trouble: damned if he does alpha and damned if he doesn't. But I see no good reason at all for thinking this possible, and good reason – lying in the role of morality in human life – for thinking it is not.[16]

At any rate, we should look at the assumption we need to make if we wish to avoid having it turn out to be possible for morality to require a person to do alpha and to not do alpha, while at the same time accepting the Thesis of Moral-Requirement. What we need to assume is clear enough: we need to assume that if refraining from doing a thing would be morally bad in a way, then it is not also the case that doing it would be morally bad in a way, and that if doing a thing would be morally bad in a way, then it is not also the case that refraining from doing it would be morally bad in a way. We need to assume, in particular, that (1) and (2) cannot both be true.

Is that plausible? *Could* it be cowardly or mean to do a thing and unjust to refrain from doing it? *Could* it be unjust to do a thing but cowardly or mean to refrain from doing it? I am inclined to think not. If doing, or refraining from doing, a thing would be unjust or cowardly or mean, then, as I think, it cannot be morally bad in any way to choose the other alternative – avoiding injustice or meanness or cowardice cannot be morally bad. I hope you will agree, since accepting the account of Moral-Requirement-Sentences that we are looking at requires that we make this assumption.[17]

---

[16] It might be worth mention that I relied on the idea that this is not possible in the preceding section, for I said there that (1_C), "Morality requires Alice to eat a banana," is false if morality requires Alice to not eat a banana.

[17] The assumption I draw attention to in the text above is first cousin of a claim discussed by Philippa Foot, namely that an act's being unjust is incompatible with its being brave or generous. See Foot (1978c). I think we should accept that claim too. In any case, it is only if we do that we can suppose – as I invited you to suppose in section 8.9 above – that there being generous and brave people in our community is good for us generally.

8.12 In chapters 6 and 7 we looked at arguments for

Moral Scepticism: It is not possible to find out about any moral sentence that it is true.

Chapter 6 attended to two epistemological arguments for that thesis; chapter 7 attended to an argument for it from premises that yield by way of intermediate conclusion that there is no such thing as having a moral belief. I suggested that none of those arguments succeed.

Even if they do not succeed, that fact certainly does not by itself entitle us to accept

Thesis of Moral Objectivity: It is possible to find out about some moral sentences that they are true.

Is it possible to find out about any moral sentences that they are true? Those who are tempted by Moral Scepticism are not going to believe that this is possible simply on the ground that the most familiar arguments for Moral Scepticism do not succeed. What is needed if they are to be convinced is an account of how we do find out about some moral sentences that they are true. In chapter 8, I have given a very rough sketch of the things that would make certain evaluatives and directives true. Since those are things we can find out about, it *is* possible to find out about some moral sentences that they are true – if the sketch is right in broad outline, or is suitably revisable, and if details can be suitably supplied.

One further matter by way of conclusion. I began by drawing attention to the fact that when people say such things as "Abortion is wrong" or "Capital punishment is unjust" we sometimes wonder whether what they said is true, and then try to find out, figure out, work out for ourselves whether it is. I called this activity Moral Assessment. But I said nothing in what followed about such complex and highly disputed issues as abortion and capital punishment. That is because my aim has not been to engage in Moral Assessment: I have wished only to make out that familiar arguments to the effect that the enterprise is pointless do not succeed (chapters 6 and 7), and to draw attention to the kinds of considerations that engaging in it requires assessment of (chapter 8). It would have been a mistake in doing those things to focus on complex and highly disputed moral issues. The existence of apparently unsettleable – at any rate, so far unsettled – moral disputes tempts people to opt for Moral Scepticism straightway. It is a good question why people suppose that there are no answers to any moral questions unless it is easy to find out what all of them are. (As if there could be no such thing as finding out any answers unless a simple algorithm is available.) But we should be clear that Moral Scepticism is false if we can find out about some moral sentences that they are true. Moral Objectivity is compatible with there being issues about which no undisputable conclusion is reached; it is compatible even with there being issues about which no undisputable conclusion is reachable.[18] Whatever the area of inquiry, whether ethics or any other, some questions raised in it can have determinate answers compatibly with there being others that do not.

[18] I know of only one work in which the possibility of moral indeterminacy is addressed head on, and a start made on an effort to accommodate it: Shafer-Landau (1994).

PART III
Responses

9

Harman's Response to Thomson's Part II

Thomson's discussion is quite impressive. She shows that the standard arguments for moral scepticism do not work and that emotivism cannot be right as an account of what ordinary people mean when they use moral language. Indeed, her arguments threaten to unravel the moral relativism I have argued for, as well as the quasi-absolutism that seemed to me compatible with my version of moral relativism. I am not sure that I can meet her challenge; but I will try. Supposing that I can meet that challenge, I then comment, from my relativistic perspective, on her constructive suggestions about how we might come to know the truth of moral conclusions.

9.1 The Thesis of Moral Objectivity

Thomson's official thesis of Moral Objectivity occurs in her Introduction:

(1) It is possible to find out about some moral sentences that they are true.

Her official statement of the contrasting thesis of Moral Scepticism, which she opposes, is therefore this.

(2) It is not possible to find out about any moral sentence
that it is true.

For the purpose of this response, I will assume that Thomson
means to count the sort of view I defended in my initial contribution to this book as an example of Moral Scepticism. So, in
particular (and this is important), I will assume a context of
extreme moral diversity in which the issue is how to decide
among different competing moral frameworks.

I will assume that she intends to count moral relativists and
Quasi-Absolutists as Moral Sceptics. But, as I will soon explain,
moral relativists and Quasi-Absolutists can accept Moral Objectivity if formulated in her official way, so the thesis needs
restatement if it is to be of any interest.

In restating the official theses, I will also replace Thomson's
phrase "moral sentences" by a phrase such as "moral claims."
We normally suppose that it is claims (or propositions, or
beliefs, or judgments, etc.) not sentences that are true or false,
since the same sentence can be used in different contexts to
make different claims with different truth values. "Alfred ought
to pay the two dollars" is true or false depending on who says
it and when it is said. I realize that talk of claims (and propositions, beliefs, judgments, etc.) can lead to difficult issues in the
philosophy of language, which neither Thomson nor I want to
address on this occasion (although maybe in the end we will
have to). Thomson's way round these issues is (I think) to take
sentences to be true or false, as used in context, with a definite
interpretation assigned to ambiguous words, to names, to indi-
cations of time in the tense of verbs, etc. In her usage, "Alfred
ought to pay the two dollars," is a different sentence when said
by you from what it is when said by me.

While I appreciate the point of that usage, my own usage has
been different, and I find that I am not quite sure how to
translate between the way I put things and the way Thomson
puts things. So, I am going to phrase my reinterpretations of her
principles in terms of claims (etc.), even though this sometimes
leads to trouble.

In any event, here's why relativists and Quasi-Absolutists will
accept Moral Objectivity as Thomson states it (1). First, a moral

relativist supposes that the truth conditions of moral claims are relative to one or another moral framework. But that is not to deny that these claims have truth conditions; and a moral relativist will suppose that it is often possible to find out that a given moral claim is true in relation to a given framework. So a moral relativist will accept (2) and will reject Thomson's version of Moral Scepticism (2), contrary to what I take to be her intentions.

Furthermore, a Quasi-Absolutist, who supposes that moral judgments are not objectively true or false, may nevertheless count moral claims as true or false in the trivial way described in section 3.3 above. So, a Quasi-Absolutist can also accept (1) and will therefore reject (2).

In order to reformulate (1) and (2) so as to give a better classification of moral relativism and Quasi-Absolutism, we might make a first attempt as follows. We begin by reformulating the thesis of Moral Objectivity as follows.

(3) Moral claims have objective truth conditions that are not relative to moral frameworks; and it is possible to find out about some of these claims that they are objectively true.

Then we can reformulate the Thesis of Moral Scepticism like this:

(4) Either moral claims do not have objective truth conditions, or their truth conditions are relative to moral frameworks, or it is not possible to find out about any of these claims that they are objectively true.

The Revised Theses (3) and (4) presuppose an understanding of what is meant by "objective truth conditions" for moral claims. As I indicated in section 3.4.1, above, I do not know how to offer a strict definition of "objective truth conditions." In that section I try to explain the relevant sort of objectivity with reference to relativism about motion.

I now turn to a further worry, namely, that the reference to "some" moral claims is far too weak. Just as it is compatible with motion relativism that certain claims about motion might be true in all spatio-temporal frameworks (e.g. that nothing travels faster than the speed of light in relation to that framework), it is compatible with moral relativism that certain moral claims might hold in relation to all moral frameworks. Consider the following claim:

> (5) In situations in which it would be morally wrong to injure another person, it would also be morally wrong to kill the other person.

A moral relativist can consistently suppose that (5) holds in relation to all moral frameworks and so in an important way is true apart from its relation to any moral framework. Furthermore, a moral relativist can consistently believe it is possible to find out that (5) is true in relation to any moral framework. But that should not count as a major concession to any interesting thesis of Moral Objectivity.

An interesting thesis must apply to more than merely "some" moral claims. And it won't help to extend (3) and (4) to "many" moral claims, since any truth has infinitely many true consequences. So, in this context, "some" automatically implies "many". But an interesting thesis needn't say that "all" moral claims can be objectively resolved. It needn't say that it is possible to find out about any moral claim whatsoever whether the claim is objectively true. Even if Moral Objectivity held in general and there were a single true morality, there would still be borderline cases in which certain moral issues had no objective resolution, just as there are nonmoral borderline cases, for example, of baldness. If I have promised to give Jack's money to the first bald person I meet, then whether or not I ought morally to give Jack's money to the person walking toward me may be a borderline case. Similarly, even if moral objectivity held in general, certain cases of abortion might be borderline cases of something's being "morally wrong." The mere existence of borderline cases is not by itself a proof of Moral Scepticism.

The real issue is the extent to which it is possible to find out the nonrelative objective truth of the sorts of moral claims that ordinary people actually make and debate. This suggests the following:

(6) The extent to which actual ordinary moral claims – claims actually made and debated by ordinary people – can be discovered to be objectively and nonrelatively true measures the extent of interesting moral objectivity.

Then the Thesis of Moral Objectivity would be:

(7) There is a relatively large extent of interesting moral objectivity.

And the Thesis of Moral Scepticism would be:

(8) There is a relatively small extent of interesting moral objectivity.

One remaining worry about these versions is that Thomson might quite reasonably want to count as a moral sceptic someone like Mackie who accepts an "error thesis" about moral claims. But Mackie might very well hold that moral claims like, "Bob ought morally to give Mary a banana," are objectively and nonrelativistically false and that their denials, for example,

(9) It is not the case that Bob ought morally to give Mary a banana

are objectively and nonrelativistically true. (7) and (8) would count an error theorist of this sort as affirming moral objectivity and denying moral scepticism!

It may seem that one way to count such an error theorist as denying moral objectivity might be to restrict (7) and (8) to "simple" or "atomic" moral claims that do not contain any embedded clauses or any logical operators like *if, and,* or *not.* However, the thought behind (9) might be expressed in a logically simpler way, for example,

(10) Bob morally may give Mary a banana.

And one kind of "error thesis" about morality holds that "Nothing is morally forbidden; everything is morally permitted; morally, you may do whatever you want." So, restricting (7) and

(8) to "simple" or "atomic" moral claims would not prevent such an error thesis from counting as affirming Moral Objectivity and denying Moral Scepticism.

This and the previous point suggest that the issues are not really best stated as issues about finding out the truth of particular moral claims. The issues really concern moral frameworks as wholes. Mackie takes every moral framework to involve error. That is the sense in which he is a Moral Sceptic. On the other hand, to go back to the previous point, finding moral claims that are acceptable in every moral framework does not help to decide among those frameworks and so does not resolve the issue posed by moral diversity. So, I suggest the following version of the Thesis of Moral Objectivity:

(11)   There is a single objectively correct moral framework, apart from vagueness and minor variation, and it is possible to find out what that moral framework is.

The corresponding version of the Thesis of Moral Scepticism is this:

(12)   Either there is no single objectively correct moral framework, even apart from vagueness and minor variation, or there is but it is not possible to find out what that moral framework is.

Further modifications are suggested below in (3) and (4).

9.2   Epistemological Arguments for Moral Scepticism

9.2.1   First Premise of the "Traditional Epistemological Argument for Moral Scepticism"

Although Thomson's crude statement of the "traditional epistemological argument for Moral Scepticism" serves quite well as background for introducing issues she wants to discuss, my own purposes are best served by taking a closer look at her formulation of the argument.

The conclusion of her "traditional argument" is her very strong

(1) It is not possible to find out about any moral sentence that it is true.

I have already observed that Moral Sceptics typically do not accept such a strong claim as (1), but, of course, if (1) could be established that would establish (12) in the preceding section as well.

But the argument as Thomson formulates it is quite defective as given. Consider the first premise.

(2) Moral sentences are not entailed by factual sentences.

One thing to notice right away is that, since any sentence (or claim) entails itself, (2) all by itself implies that moral sentences are not factual, which implies they cannot be objectively true and so cannot be known to be objectively true.

To avoid this blatant begging of the question, we might follow tradition and try replacing "factual" with "descriptive" (also replacing "sentence" with "claim" as previously discussed):

(3) Moral claims are not entailed by descriptive claims.

But can we distinguish moral claims from descriptive claims in a way that satisfies (3)? Not if all claims have to be classified as either descriptive or moral and the denial of a descriptive claim is also a descriptive claim.

The point is a matter of elementary logic (Prior 1976). Suppose that D is a descriptive claim (e.g. "Bob gave Mary a banana") and M is a moral claim (e.g. "Bob ought to give Mary a banana"). Then consider the claim $(D \lor M)$ – the inclusive disjunction, *either D or M or both* ("Either Bob gave Mary a banana or Bob ought to give Mary a banana"). The problem is that, if the disjunction $(D \lor M)$ is a moral claim, then it is a moral claim that is entailed by the descriptive claim *D*. But, if the disjunction *(D v M)* is a descriptive claim, then it and the descriptive claim *not-D* ("Bob did not give Mary a banana") together entail the moral claim *M*. Either way, a moral claim is entailed by a descriptive claim.

It might be suggested that one way to avoid this result would be to adopt a suggestion already mentioned in discussing (7) and (8), namely to restrict the premise to "simple" or "atomic" moral claims. Then we can count *(D v M)* as a moral claim and agree that it is entailed by the descriptive claim *D* but observe that *(D v M)* is not a simple or atomic moral claim.

This may avoid the one logical problem but a related problem remains, namely, that, at least in standard logics, inconsistent claims imply anything. So, in particular, inconsistent descriptive claims imply simple atomic moral claims. Here's a short two-step argument from the inconsistent descriptive claims *D* and *not-D* to the simple atomic moral claim *M: D* implies *(D v M)*; *(D v M)* and *not-D* imply *M*.

In responding to the problem raised by inconsistent premises, it is useful to recall that the issue as Thomson sees it is how to find out whether a given moral claim is true. We are not going to find out whether *M* is true by finding out that both *D* and *not-D* are true and then noticing that *D* and *not-D* entail *M*. We cannot find out that both *D* and *not-D* are true, because we cannot find out that something is true unless it is true and it cannot happen that both *D* and *not-D* are true.

So, it seems reasonable to replace (3) with

(4) Simple or atomic moral claims are not entailed by descriptive claims that we can find out to be true.

9.2.2 Second Premise of "The Traditional Epistemological Argument for Moral Scepticism"

Now let us consider the second premise of the "traditional epistemological argument" as Thomson presents it, making appropriate changes to fit our revised version of her first premise.

(5) The only way we have of finding out that a simple or atomic moral claim is true is by finding out that certain descriptive claims are true, and drawing the moral claim as conclusion from them.

As stated, (5) – like (2), the original form of the first premise – already itself assumes Moral Scepticism. Consider reaching the conclusion

(6) I ought morally to pay Bob ten dollars

by inferring it from the two premises

(7) I ought morally to pay Bob ten dollars if he asks me to.

(8) Bob has just asked me to pay him ten dollars.

If I cannot find out that (6) is true via such an inference, that can only be because I cannot know the premises are true. In this context, it is assumed that I can know that (8) is true. So, in this context, (5) amounts to the assumption that I cannot know that (7) is true. But to assume that I cannot know that (7) is true is to assume Moral Scepticism for this case.

The Sceptic might ask how I can know (7) is true. If I infer (7) from other things and if any of those other premises are moral claims, the question arises how I know them. Ultimately, according to one view of the matter, I am going to have to depend on only descriptive premises. This suggests replacing (5) with

(9) Ultimately, our knowledge of the truth of a simple or atomic moral claim must rest on an inference from descriptive claims that we have discovered to be true.

In this view, although we may in the first instance come to find out that a moral claim is true by inferring it from some other moral claim along with a descriptive claim, our knowledge of the truth of the moral claim, if we have it, ultimately rests on an inference from descriptive claims alone, according to (9).

9.2.3 *Foundations Theory of Knowledge*

Reflection along similar lines is sometimes taken to motivate a so-called "foundations" theory of knowledge. In this view, knowledge ultimately has to be inferred from foundational knowledge that is known without inference. Foundational knowledge might be either intuitive (*Everything is identical with itself*) or observational (*I seem to be seeing something red*). This suggests replacing (9) with

> (10) Ultimately, our knowledge of the truth of a simple or atomic moral claim must rest on a justification from a basis of intuitive and observational foundational claims that we have discovered to be true without inference.

The third premise in our reconstructed traditional epistemological argument for Moral Scepticism would then amount to the claim that there is a justification of a claim *C* from a foundational basis *B* only if *B* entails *C*. But since it is clear that justification should not be restricted to entailment, we should replace both (4) and the third premise with a single premise:

> (11) Simple or atomic moral claims cannot be justified on the basis of intuitive and observational foundation claims that we have found out to be true without inference.

(10) and (11) together imply the strong form of Moral Scepticism in (1).

9.2.4 *Problems with Foundationalism*

Two kinds of problems arise for this sort of appeal to foundationalism. First, there are problems about what count as relevant foundations. General views and theories affect observations and determine intuitions. People who accept a given moral framework treat certain moral principles of that framework as intuitively correct, e.g. *It is morally wrong to tell a lie*. People who accept a given moral framework make morally loaded observational judgments that accord with the framework: seeing some kids setting fire to a cat, someone might arrive at the judgment, *What they are doing is wrong*, immediately and without any conscious inference. If these count as foundational claims, (11) is clearly refuted, since claims that are part of the foundation are automatically justified on the basis of that foundation (at least in the absence of specific challenges to those claims arising from other foundational beliefs). On the other hand, if these claims do not count as foundational claims, it becomes quite unclear what can count. In any event, *such* intuitions and observations are not going to be able to settle issues between moral frameworks, since one person's intuition is another person's prejudice.

Second, there are problems about the accessibility of a justification to the person whose knowledge is grounded in that justification. Must the person have consciously reasoned in a certain way at some point? Is the justification something the person can now produce? Can people produce philosophically acceptable justifications for the claims we would normally take them to know? If someone does not have an acceptable justification for a claim, should that person abandon belief in that claim? In fact people typically do not keep track of their reasons or justification for their beliefs. Does this mean that people should abandon almost everything they believe?

In ordinary life we suppose that special reasons are needed to justify *changing* your mind and that special reasons are not needed to justify keeping your mind unchanged in the absence of a special reason to change your mind. Normally, you don't need reasons to continue to believe what you already believe. You must begin reasoning from where you are now, not from some distant and imaginary foundation of observation and intuition. Any reasons you might have to abandon a present belief would have to come from other beliefs of yours. What you are justified in believing depends on what you already believe.

This means that people with very different moral outlooks may be justified in their moral views and may be justified in taking themselves to know various moral truths. Moral Scepticism is quite compatible with this possibility, just as scepticism about absolute motion is quite compatible with people being justified in their local beliefs about motion. The issue of Moral Scepticism does not arise as a serious issue until the fact of moral diversity is fully appreciated. Only then is there a special reason to consider the possibility that Moral Relativism may hold, a reason to ask how we might decide among the competing moral frameworks revealed by actual moral diversity. We may discover that there is no objective ground for favoring one framework over another, just as we discover that there is no objective ground for favoring one spatio-temporal framework over another for determining whether something is really in motion.

9.2.5 *Moral Explanations of Nonmoral Facts*

In science, competition among theories come sometimes be settled by testing the theories against observation, that is, by finding observations that can be more easily explained by one theory than by its competitors. So, one important issue with respect to Moral Objectivity and Moral Scepticism is whether competition among moral frameworks can be tested in this way.

This is the issue Thomson discusses when she discusses the claim

(12) There is no moral sentence whose truth would explain the truth of a factual sentence.

To see that competition among moral frameworks is what is at issue, observe that a crucial part of what may look like an argument she gives for (12) is really an argument for

(13) No observation (or other fact not in dispute between moral frameworks) is better explained by one moral framework than by others in a way that would provide evidence for the one moral framework as compared with the others.

This occurs in Thomson's discussion of what she calls "STUR-GEON PICTURE OF ALICE" (in section 7.5). We are to

> suppose that Alice had given her word that she would give Bert a banana, and that she did so, despite the fact that it was costly for her to do so and she could have got away with not doing so.

Thomson raises the question whether in this case

> (14) Alice's being just would explain her giving Bert the banana.

Her answer is that,

> for the purposes of a person who wishes to rebut the no-explanation argument for Moral Scepticism, there is less in this case... than meets the eye.

She then observes that any such explanation requires the assumption that Alice's acting as she acted was just.

But what entitles us to assume that Alice's giving Bert a banana was just? She then rejects the explanation because we are not in this context entitled to make such an assumption.

Notice that Thomson does not actually argue against the explanatory claim (14). She argues rather that "a person who wishes to rebut the no-explanation argument for Moral Scepticism" is not entitled to appeal to (14). Her point is well taken, it seems to me.

We are concerned with whether there is anything that can be better explained by one moral framework than by another in a way that provides evidence for the one framework as compared with the other. Although the fact that Alice gave Bert a banana might be explained by the hypothesis that Alice is just and it is just for her to give Bert a banana, the same fact is equally well explained on the weaker assumptions that Alice is disposed to do things that are just in relation to a certain moral framework and that it is just in relation to that framework for her to give Bert a banana. In a context in which it is a matter of controversy whether Alice is just and a matter of controversy whether it is just for Alice to give Bert a banana, Alice's giving Bert a banana is evidence neither that she was just nor that it is just for her to do so.

In a scientific dispute it is sometimes possible to find evidence that is better explained by one of the competing theories in a way that provides decisive evidence in favor of that theory. The fact that Alice gives Burt a banana is not in the same way decisive evidence in favor of a particular controversial conception of justice.

Similar remarks hold of the other cases Thomson discusses. Whether or not they are cases in which a moral claim explains some uncontroversial facts, they are not cases that support one moral framework as compared with another.

9.2.6 Might other Evidence Favor one Moral Framework over another?

Thomson argues that it is not "a disaster for friends of Moral Objectivity" to have to accept the results of the last section. But maybe it is a disaster.

After pointing out, correctly, that there can be evidence for a claim that explains the claim and is not explained by the claim, Thomson offers the following putative moral example:

(15) Alice's giving Bert a banana involved her keeping her word when it cost her a lot to do so and she could have got away with not doing so. That would explain and is evidence or the conclusion that Alice's giving Bert a banana was just.

But (15) serves no better than the suggestion we have just considered, that Alice's giving Bert a banana is evidence that Alice is just because her being just would explain her giving Bert a banana. Just as the earlier suggestion is ruled out on the grounds that "a person who wishes to rebut the no-explanation argument for Moral Scepticism" is not entitled to appeal to the suggested explanation of Alice's behavior, so is (15). Clearly, in a context of a dispute as to whether actions like Alice's constitute justice, the last sentence in (15) is controversial and cannot show that there is evidence in favor of one moral framework rather than another.

It is not evidence for a theory *T* that, according to *T*, certain undisputed facts would explain the truth of certain contested theoretical conclusion that follows from *T* but not from the competing theories. It is evidence for a theory *T* that *T* would allow a better explanation of certain undisputed facts than would competing theories. That's why it is relevant for Moral Objectivity to consider what sort of explanations a given moral framework might provide of undisputed facts but not relevant to consider what contested moral conclusions a given framework would take to be explained by undisputed facts.

9.3 Emotivism

9.3.1 Thomson's Account of Emotivism

The view I called "Quasi-Absolutism" is a kind of Emotivism. Since the possibility of Quasi-Absolutism complicates the statement of moral relativism, I am interested in Thomson's discussion of Emotivism for any light it might shed on the tenability of Quasi-Absolutism.

Thomson identifies Emotivism with a cluster of theses, the first of which is

(1) Moral sentences have no truth values.

This formulation is troublesome for a reason already mentioned, namely, that in general it is claims (or propositions or beliefs, etc.) that have truth value, not sentences. Consider the sentence, "Bob gave Alice a banana." That sentence, as a sentence, has no truth value, apart from a context that helps to specify which Bob and Alice are being referred to and what the reference time is in relation to which the giving is supposed to be in the past.

On the other hand, Thomson's Emotivist might be reluctant to suppose there are moral "claims" or "propositions" or "beliefs." One of the Emotivists she refers to, R. M. Hare, takes moral sentences to be disguised imperatives; and imperatives are not normally used to make claims or express beliefs. To mention one of her examples, the sentence, "Go to the store!" is not used to make a claim or express a belief.

On the other hand, consider the moral sentence, "I have a moral right to this banana." Presumably, even an Emotivist might count that as "making a claim," in this case a claim to a banana, but perhaps not a claim with a truth value. This suggests a revision:

> (2) Moral sentences are not used to make claims with truth values.

Thomson says that "if the No-Truth-Value Thesis is correct, so also is Moral Scepticism, for if no moral sentences have truth-values, then none are true, and a fortiori it is not possible to find out about any that they are true." But some defenders of the imperative analysis of moral sentences don't seem to be Moral Sceptics. Immanuel Kant, Alan Gewirth, and R. M. Hare all suppose that acceptance of certain imperatives is rationally required of all rational beings who think carefully enough. It seems wrong to count them as moral sceptics. Even though Thomson is right to say that they cannot hold that it is possible to find out that moral claims are true, perhaps we can say that these philosophers suppose that it is possible to find out that certain moral claims are "valid." So, we need to further revise our account of Moral Objectivity as follows.

> (3) Moral claims or imperatives have objective truth or validity conditions that are not relative to moral frameworks; and it is possible to find out about some of these claims or imperatives that they are objectively true or valid.

Then our account of Moral Scepticism becomes this:

(4) Either moral claims or imperatives do not have objective truth or validity conditions, or their truth or validity conditions are relative to moral frameworks, or it is not possible to find out about any of these claims or imperatives that they are objectively true or valid.

Another thing Thomson says is that the No-Truth-Value Thesis implies

(5) There are no moral facts.

But a defender of the imperative analysis of moral sentences could say that the fact that a certain moral imperative is valid for all rational beings is a moral fact even though it is not expressed by a moral sentence. So, the No-Truth-Value Thesis, represented either as (1) or as (2), does not imply the No-Fact Thesis (5).

Thomson also says, controversially, that "nothing could entail what lacks a truth-value." This is controversial, first, because some philosophers have argued that there are entailments involving imperatives. For example, it is a possible view that "Give Alice a banana!" follows from, "You promised to give Alice a banana" and "Keep your promises!"

Second, many philosophical logicians suppose that claims that lack truth value because they involve false presuppositions can be entailed by other claims. For example, many philosophical logicians hold that "The present King of France is bald" has no truth value because both it and its seeming denial, "The present King of France is not bald," presuppose falsely that there is a present King of France. They might also hold that "The present King of France is bald" is entailed by "Either the present King of France is bald or the present Queen of England is bald" and "The present Queen of England is not bald." One version of an "error thesis" takes moral claims to involve a false presupposition, e.g. of Moral Absolutism. In this version, moral claims are neither true nor false, even though entailments can hold among them.

Returning to our revision of the No-Truth-Value Thesis (2), we need to make two further changes. First, an Emotivist need not deny the possibility of using moral sentences to make relational moral claims with truth values. What the Emotivist says is that there is another, nonrelational way to use moral sentences, emotivism being a claim about that usage. Second, if some form of Quasi-Absolutism is correct, we can attribute trivial truth-conditions to such remarks in a way I tried to explain in chapter 3, although the truth conditions are not objective truth conditions. So, we might revise (2) as follows.

(6) Moral sentences can be used to make absolute judgments that are not relative to one or another moral framework, but such judgments do not have objective truth values.

Similarly, the No-Fact Thesis (5) should be formulated as a claim about objective facts.

(7) There are no objective moral facts apart from a relation to one or another moral framework.

Thomson takes Emotivism to involve two other theses. The first is a Speech-Act Thesis.

(8) One who asserts a moral sentence merely displays an attitude, pro or con.

Again, since Emotivism does not have to rule out the moral relativist's usage, this needs to be restricted to someone who intends to be making a nonrelative judgment. Furthermore, Emotivism need not make a claim about the intentions of all such speakers. Some may be intending to say something about objective nonrelative moral reality. To repeat, emotivism, at least as I understand it, is a view about a possible use of moral sentences; it need not deny there are other possible uses. So, we might consider a Revised Speech-Act Thesis:

(9) There is an intelligible use of moral terminology in which one who asserts a moral sentence merely displays an attitude, pro or con.

There are still problems. (9) does not cover the imperative theory, which I assume Thomson counts as a form of Emotivism. Perhaps, "Keep your promises!" expresses a pro-attitude toward promise keeping, but it does not merely display such an attitude in the way that "Hooray for promise keeping!" does. Imperatives are different from exclamations.

Furthermore, as Thomson observes in a footnote in section 7.5 many cases of permission display neither a pro-attitude nor a con-attitude, for example, "Bob may keep his banana; he is not morally required to give it to Mary; he needn't do so". Any version of Emotivism needs to say something about such judgments but does not have to say that a pro-attitude or con-attitude is always involved. The Quasi-Absolutism I was worried about has something to say about such judgments, for example.

The example just given shows that it will not work merely to restrict the Speech-Act Thesis to simple, atomic moral judgments, because "Bob may keep his banana" surely counts as such a judgment.

In order to avoid these difficulties, we might try a further revision.

(10)   There is an intelligible use of moral terminology in which one who asserts a simple, atomic moral sentence indicating that someone ought morally to do something, that a certain course of action is or would be wrong, etc. displays an attitude, pro or con.

Ideally, the "etc." would be more fully specified in this principle.

Some of the points I have made about the Speech-Act Thesis, apply to the final thesis Thomson attributes to Emotivism, the No-Moral-Belief Thesis.

(11)   There is no such thing as having a moral belief – being in the state that we (mistakenly) call "having a moral belief" is merely having an attitude, pro or con.

Emotivism should allow for relativistic beliefs as well as for mistaken beliefs about nonrelative moral reality. Emotivism should not say that what we call "having a moral belief" is "merely" having an attitude. Emotivism must allow for cases in which the relevant attitude is neither pro nor con, as when one thinks that Bob may keep his banana.

Furthermore, there is no reason to restrict the term "belief" in the way the No-Moral-Belief Thesis does. We can count the relevant attitude as a moral belief. There is no need to suppose that this is a "mistaken" use of the term "belief." (Similarly, it is not a mistaken use of the term "belief" to say that I believe in my students.)

Making appropriate revisions yields:

> (12) There is a kind of moral belief for which having the belief that some particular action is morally wrong or that a particular person ought to do a given thing, etc., is having a certain attitude, pro or con, to something.

I would also suggest, as a further key point distinguishing the Emotivist usage from a Moral Absolutist usage of moral terms, that a speaker may use Emotivist (Quasi-Absolutist) moral language to assert (and believe) a moral claim without taking it to be an objective matter whether the claim is correct. With respect to speech-acts, we have:

> (13) There is an intelligible use of moral terminology in which one can displays an attitude, pro or con, by sincerely asserting a moral sentence without supposing it is an objective matter whether one's assertion is correct.

With respect to moral belief, we have:

> (14) Having a moral belief is sometimes a matter of having a certain attitude, pro or con, to something without supposing that it is an objective matter whether one's belief is correct.

9.3.2 Thomson's Objections to Spirit Emotivism

In moving from Thomson's emotivist theses (1), (5), (8), and (11) to my versions (6), (7), (10), (12), (13), and (14), I have moved from what she calls "Letter-Emotivism" to a version what she calls "Spirit-Emotivism," a view she says is "a mistake that issues largely from failing to take the richness of moral thinking seriously enough" (section 7.5).

In particular, she asks how one is to be specific about the relevant pro and con attitudes associated with various particular moral judgments, such as "Alice ought to give Bert a banana," "Alice ought not to give Bert a banana," "It would be fair for Alice to give Bert a banana," "Alice is just," and "Alice is brave." What attitudes are in question and what are they attitudes toward? Thomson doubts that a satisfactory answer can be given to these questions (section 7.4).

One possible answer (suggested in section 3.2, above) is that the relevant attitude is in the first instance an attitude of approval of a certain moral framework. A moral judgment combines a judgment, e.g., that Alice is just in relation to the standards of moral framework *M*, together with approval of those standards. The relevant approval might involve a disposition to approve of acts that are in accord with those standards, a disposition to try to act oneself in accord with the standards, and a disposition to desire to be the sort of person with the virtues endorsed by those standards. In this view, we do not need to find a different pro or con attitudes for each kind of moral judgment. Differences in moral judgment are to be accounted for the different roles these judgments play in a given moral framework.

Can there be a coherent use of language subject to these conditions? Consider Thomson's indifferent character, Jones, whom she discusses in 7.9. Cannot Jones make Quasi-Absolutist judgments in relation to moral framework *M*, even though Jones does not care about moral framework *M* or any other moral framework in the relevant way? Jones has no disposition to approve of acts simply because they are in accord with the standards of *M*; Jones has no disposition to try to act in accord with those standards; and Jones has no disposition to desire to be the sort of person with the virtues endorsed by those standards. Jones's concern with these moral judgments reflects a mere "idle curiosity," as Thomson says.

Jones's usage of the relevant moral terminology might relevantly coincide with Smith's usage, where Smith consciously uses this terminology as QA terminology in part to express his approval of moral framework *M*. In other words Jones makes the same judgments as Smith and, like Smith, Jones does not treat these judgments as relational judgments; Jones, like Smith, uses this terminology to express (what Jones takes to be) disagreement with speakers whose judgments derive from different moral frameworks.

If Jones's moral terminology has the same meaning as Smith's, then it is or would seem to be irrelevant to the meaning of words used in this way that the words are used to express approval of some moral framework. So, it would seem that Quasi-Absolutists must deny that Jones can give this terminology the same meaning as Smith, even though the two of them can converse with each other without any confusion.

However, the fact that two people can converse with each other without confusion need not show that they assign the same meaning to what they are saying. A moral relativist and Quasi-Absolutist can have perfectly ordinary conversations with a regular moral absolutist, as long as the first two speakers make their judgments in relation to the same moral framework lying behind the absolutist's judgments, just as a motion relativist can have perfectly ordinary conversations about motion with a motion absolutist, as long as these conversations concern motion in relation to the framework that the motion absolutist takes to be privileged.

What does Jones mean by moral terminology? The story so far is compatible with Jones using this terminology in an absolutist way. To block that interpretation, we might add that Jones, like Smith, supposes that there is no objective truth to moral issues.

But then it does become quite obscure to me what Jones could possibly take himself to be saying when he makes a moral judgment. It would no longer be clear in what sense his interest in the answers can be conceived as idle curiosity. Can one be curious about something that one takes to have no objective answer?

Alternatively, we can imagine that Jones, like most people, simply has no view about what he is doing. He has simply picked up moral terminology from others in his society. The sense in which he doesn't suppose there are objective answers to moral issues is simply that he has no view on this question; he simply hasn't thought about it; or, if he has thought about it, he doesn't know what the answer is. Perhaps that is enough for him to indulge in idle curiosity about the answers to moral questions.

In such a case, we might suppose that Jones's words borrow their meaning from the same words as used by others in the society. In that case, Jones uses the QA terminology even though he does not use it to approve of a given morality.

The QA theorist might still take such approval to be crucial to the use of such terminology, treating Jones's usage is derivative from the use by others in which the terminology to express such approval. (Similarly, the meaning of Jones's word "arthritis" might be derivative from the way other people use the term and may therefore depend on beliefs about arthritis that Jones himself does not possess (see, e.g., Burge 1986).)

At this point we encounter large issues in the philosophy of language that I cannot pursue further. For now, I conclude that Thomson's discussion of emotivism does not show that moral terminology cannot be used in the way suggested by Quasi-Absolutism.

9.4 Good

In chapter 8, Thomson sketches how certain normative questions might be given what she takes to be objective answers. In section 8.2, she expresses sympathy with the view that nothing is ever good period; it is always good in one or another way. Furthermore, the ways in which things are good are not always comparable, so it does not make sense to ask whether Alice's Mercedes is better than [the taste of] chocolate. She mentions five such ways in which something can be good: being useful or good for use in doing something, being skillful or good at doing something, being enjoyable or good to experience, being beneficial or good for something, and being morally good in one or another way. I will begin by considering her account of the nonmoral cases. Then I will discuss her account of ways of being morally good. In each case I will argue for a relativism that goes beyond any that she acknowledges.

9.4.1 *Usefulness and Skillfulness*

Thomson's discussion of usefulness culminates in the following, "Usefulness Generalization":

(1) Being good for use in X-ing consists in being such as to facilitate X-ing in manners that conduce to satisfying the wants people typically X to satisfy.

She observes that the wants people typically X to satisfy in "this world" may differ from the wants people typically X to satisfy in some other world, so there is an implicit relativity here to this world or to what is typically wanted in this world. But I think a greater relativity is called for.

The wants people typically X to satisfy in one place in this world may differ from the wants people typically X to satisfy in another place in this world. Surely, the wants that are typical in one place should not determine what is good for use in X-ing in the other place, even if there are more people in the first place than the second, so that the first wants count as typical. Furthermore, there may be two groups of people intermixed in a given place. The fact that one group is larger than the other should not determine what it is good for use in X-ing by members of the other group.

Finally, it can happen that individuals vary in the wants they X to satisfy. Sometimes they X to satisfy some wants, sometimes they X to satisfy other quite different wants. What is good for use in X-ing should similarly vary with these wants. So, we need to replace (1) with

(2) Being good for use in X-ing is relative to certain wants W that are to be satisfied by X-ing and consists in being such as to facilitate X-ing in manners that conduce to satisfying W.

For the same reason, Thomson's "Skillfulness Generalization,"

   (3) Being good at X-ing consists in being capable of X-ing in the manner that people who want to X typically want to X in,

needs to be relativized as follows:

   (4) Being good at X-ing is relative to certain wants W concerning the manner in which to X and consists in being capable of X-ing in the manner that satisfy W.

9.4.2 Taste

With respect to what tastes good, is good to look at, etc., Thomson suggests we need to appeal to experts. For good paintings and good wine, she states these principles.

   (5) A K's being good to look at consists in its being such as to please, by its looks, those who are experts in Ks.

   (6) A K's tasting good consists in its being such as to please, by its taste, those who are experts in Ks.

Good music might be covered by an analogous principle:

   (7) A K's sounding good consists in its being such as to please, by its sound, those who are experts in Ks.

She suggests that experts in Ks can be identified in terms of their broad acquaintance with Ks, their abilities to make distinctions among Ks, etc.

But this approach requires the assumption, so to speak, that experts in Ks all have the same taste in Ks. Surely, that assumption is patently false. Experts in art differ greatly in what they like about the artworks in which they are expert. Similarly for experts in every other field. Furthermore, it is well known that there are constant changes in critical taste from time to time, from place to place, from person to person, and even from one moment to another in a given person, with changes in the person's aesthetic sensibility.

I take myself to be fairly expert concerning jazz, but what sorts of jazz I find pleasing varies from day to day and over the course of any single day. I do not think I am in any way unusual in this respect.

Such considerations suggest a relativistic account of such judgments of taste:

> (8) A K's sounding good is relative to a certain sensibility S and consists in K's being such as to please, by its sound, those who have sensibility S.

And similarly for "tasting good," and "looking good."

If anything like this is correct, expertise is relevant only to the extent that it may be needed for possession of a given aesthetic sensibility.

9.4.3 Benefit and Well-being

With respect to what's beneficial to something, Thomson (section 8.8) offers the following account:

> (9) X's being good for Y consists in X's being conductive to Y's welfare, or to Y's being in good condition, or anyway to Y's being in better condition that it would otherwise be.

For artifacts she suggests something like

> (10) If Ks are manufactured articles, then a K's being in good condition is for it to be in the condition such that people who want a K typically want a K in that condition.

Since different people may want Ks in different conditions, this is best relativized to such wants:

(11) If Ks are manufactured articles, then a K's being in good condition is relative to certain wants *W* for a K in a certain condition and consists in its being in the sort of condition wanted by *W*.

I pass over her inconclusive discussion of plants and animals. With respect to the important case of people, her view is this.

(12) A person's well-being consists in his or her life's going as he or she wants it to go, subject to constraints of two kinds. On the one hand, the life the person is leading has to have been chosen in awareness of its costs, including opportunity costs. On the other hand, the choice has to have been autonomously made...

She adds persuasively that these constraints are "less strict than they are sometimes said to be."

Apart from such details, (12) is clearly controversial in defining welfare solely in terms of the satisfaction of the individual's desires.

Consider Tom, who leads an ordinary life of a certain sort. It seem to me that, if Tom had led pretty much the same life except for having more or fewer goals, his well-being would have been much the same, as long as he was not upset by not having achieved the goals in question. (12) implies that he would have had less well-being if he had had more goals, if the additional goals had not been satisfied, even if he was not upset by their failure to be satisfied.

To take another example, many people believe that a person's life goes less well if the person lacks certain experiences, for example, experiences of music. If the person simply does not care about music, then that lack of concern for music is itself a loss to that person, even though the person is not aware of it as a loss.

It is widely believed that a life without friends tends to be a poor life, again, even if the person in question does not care to have friends. The person's life may satisfy his or her desires so there is no way in terms of (12) to count the absence of friends as affecting the person's welfare.

A conception of human welfare typically involves specific goods of a more controversial sort, for example, having a family of a certain sort, being a person of courage, having certain skills, etc., where the details vary from one conception to another. The idea is not just that such things are good for those that want them, but that they are good for anyone, and that failure to want them is itself a loss. Thomson's conception of human welfare is one among many.

In some conceptions, the "good life" includes the discriminating enjoyment of good meat and wine; in other conceptions no life can count as a good life if it involves the exploitation of animals raised for food. Some conceptions take the good life to involve at its core the pursuit of an individual project of excellence; some conceptions take the good life to involve service to others. Some conceptions of the good life stress the importance of elaborate social rituals of politeness; in others such rituals are trivialities of no importance at all to the good life. Different conceptions put different weights on the joys of combat and competition as against the benefits of cooperation and shared undertakings. They disagree on the relative importance of knowledge and culture as compared with pleasure and simple happiness.

Is there a single correct conception of human welfare? Consideration of cases suggests a relativistic answer here, as in morality more generally.

(13) Human welfare is relative to certain standards *S*. A life goes well in relation to *S* to the extent that it satisfies *S*.

But full discussion of this issue would involve another book!

9.4.4 Moral Goodness

According to Thomson (section 8.9),

Just as there is no (pure, unadulterated) goodness, so also is there no (pure, unadulterated) moral goodness. Everything that is good

is good-in-a-way; so also is everything that is morally good morally-good-in-a-way – generous, or brave, or just, or considerate,
and so on.

But the point about moral goodness does not really parallel the
earlier point about goodness. In the earlier case, we had to add
a qualification to "good" to get "good for X-ing" "good at X-
ing," "good to experience," and "good for X," whereas in the
present case the point seems to be merely that an act can be
morally good only by virtue of having one or another feature by
virtue of which it is morally good, some (morally) good-making
feature.

The former case concerned the evaluation of different sorts of
things – usefulness, skill, etc. The present case is concerned
with the moral evaluation of a single sort of thing, namely, an
action.

In the former case, Thomson made her case in part by noting
that that it is confused to compare how good a particular hammer is for use in hammering with how good a particular person
is at hammering. In the present case, however, it would seem to
make sense at least sometimes to compare the moral worth of a
particular act of generosity with the moral worth of a particular
act of bravery. For example, it seems an intelligible thought that
acts of bravery tend to be morally better acts than acts of
generosity.

Indeed, it is commonly supposed that the way to morally
evaluate a possible act is to compare the morally good-making
(or right-making) characteristics the act would have with the
morally bad-making (or wrong-making) characteristics the act
would have. It the former characteristics are weightier than the
latter, the act would be morally good or right; if the latter
characteristics are weightier than the former, the act would be
morally bad or wrong.

Suppose Mary has made independent promises to Nancy,
Oscar, and Paul. Each promise is equally serious and matters
equally to the person to whom it was made. It turns out that
Mary cannot keep all three promises. She can either keep her
promises to Nancy and Oscar but not her promise to Paul, or she
can keep her promise to Paul but not Oscar or Nancy. If she

takes the first course of action, she acts justly to Nancy and Oscar and unjustly to Paul. If instead she takes the second course of action, she acts justly to Paul but unjustly to Nancy and Oscar. In this case, the standard view is that it would be morally better for her to take the first course of action than the second, so that is the course of action she *ought* morally to take.

Thomson is committed to rejecting that view of what Mary is faced with. Thomson accepts the following "Thesis of Moral Requirement" (section 3.11).

(14)   A person is morally required to do a thing just in case his or her refraining from doing the thing would be morally bad in some way – mean or cowardly or unjust and so on.

Furthermore, she also accepts the following principle.

(15)   It is never true both that a person is morally required to do something and also morally required not to do it.

According to the story about Mary, if she takes the first course of action she acts unjustly to Paul, but if she does not she acts unjustly to Nancy and Oscar. According to (14) that means Mary is morally required to take the first course of action and also morally require not to take that course of action. But (15) says such a conclusion is never true. So, these two principles rule out the story told about Mary.

9.4.5 *Relativity of Moral Goodness*

In any event, Thomson seems to believe that questions of moral requirement reduce to or are at least importantly dependent on questions of the moral goodness of acts, where that is always a matter of an act's being courageous or cowardly, mean or generous, just or unjust, and so on. Supposing that she is right, there are still the same reasons for moral relativism that I mentioned in chapter 1, for there is as much moral diversity concerning when an act has any of these sorts of characteristics as there is concerning what moral rules are to be accepted. Is it unjust to raise animals for food? Is it unfair not to help a dying person who in great pain to die? Is it mean to purchase a new record player instead of trying to help people who cannot afford food? Is it courageous to risk one's life to save the lives of strangers or is it merely stupid and imprudent?

In addition, of course, different moral frameworks will recognize different moral virtues, different ways of being morally good or bad. Is sexual promiscuity a moral fault? Is reverence toward God a moral virtue?

The apparent intractability of these and other moral issues provides evidence for moral relativism that is in certain ways similar to the evidence we have for spatio-temporal relativity. But I will not try here to repeat the argument of chapter 1.

9.5 Conclusion

Thomson's chapters 6–8 show that Moral Scepticism cannot be plausibly defended merely by comparing features of moral language with features of nonmoral discourse. Moral diversity and the apparent intractability of moral disagreements provide the evidence for Moral Scepticism and ultimately for Moral Relativism. Given Moral Relativism, Quasi-Absolutism appears to provide a coherent way to mimic Moral Absolutism from within Moral Relativism. This makes it difficult to formulate Moral Relativism; but an adequate formulation is possible if we can rely on a notion of Objectivity as in (3) of 3.4.1.

10

Thomson's Response to Harman's Part I

10.1 Harman's lively and interesting chapters 1–5 cover a lot of ground; I regret that I have space to comment on only two of the theses he advances.

He calls the first Moral Relativism. It says, among other things:

> For the purposes of assigning truth conditions, a judgment of the form *it would be morally wrong of P to D*, has to be understood as elliptical for a judgment of the form, *in relation to moral framework M, it would be morally wrong of P to D*. Similarly for other moral judgments. (sec. 1. 1)

(He tells us that this is merely "a first approximation" to the thesis in the offing here; I will comment briefly on his revision of it in section 10.7 below.) I take Harman to have four things in mind. The first is that moral sentences have no truth-values. For example, the moral sentence

(S) It would be morally wrong of Paul to engage in dancing

has no truth-value. The second is that certain nonmoral sentences constructible from moral sentences do have truth-values. Let us give moral frameworks names: Mark, Matthew, Michael,

Morgan, and so on. Then while (S), being a moral sentence, has no truth-value,

(T) In relation to Mark, it would be morally wrong of Paul to engage in dancing,

and

> In relation to Matthew, it would be morally wrong of Paul to engage in dancing,

and so on, are not moral sentences, and do have truth-values. What are the relations between moral sentences such as (S) and nonmoral sentences such as (T)? Harman says that "for the purposes of assigning truth conditions," moral sentences have "to be understood as elliptical for" sentences constructible from them in the way he indicated. But he says that we are not to be misled by his use of the word "elliptical." Suppose Paula asserted (S). It might have been moral framework Mark that was "conspicuous" or "salient" to her at the time. But we are not to take Harman to be claiming that when Paula asserted (S) she meant (T). We are not to take him to be claiming that when she asserted (S) she was thereby asserting that in relation to Mark, it would be morally wrong of Paul to engage in dancing.[1] For he says: "Moral relativism does not claim that people intend their

---

[1] Another way of expressing the point here is this: we are not to take Harman to be claiming that when Paula asserted the *sentence* (S) she was thereby asserting the *proposition* expressed by (T). As I say in the text above, that is not Harman's idea.

It is an idea that has been held by other people, however, people who also call themselves moral relativists. As is indicated by my parenthetical remark in the text below ("Surely they don't intend this!"), my own view is that Harman is right to reject the idea. If you want to be a moral relativist, I recommend Harman's version, which is subtler than its competitors. In any case, it is Harman's version of moral relativism that I will be concerned with throughout. To mark its distinctiveness, I use capital letters – that is, I call it "Moral Relativism."

In passing, I should say that it was for the sake of clarity that in summarizing Harman's view I replaced his word "judgment" by the word "sentence." Many people use "judgment" as an alternative to "proposition," but propositions by definition have truth-values, and it is Harman's view that what he calls "a judgment of the form *it would be morally wrong of P to D*" lacks a truth-value.

moral judgments to be 'elliptical' in the suggested way." (Surely they don't intend this!) So how does Harman think moral sentences such as (S) are related to nonmoral sentences such as (T)? Harman's thesis does not itself make this clear.

In light of his discussion of the thesis in the text that surrounds it, I think we can summarize his answer as follows. Moral sentences such as (S) are in a certain way incomplete; indeed, it is because moral sentences such as (S) are incomplete in that way that they lack truth-values. That is the third thing I take him to have in mind. Nonmoral sentences such as (T) are completions of moral sentences; so moral sentences such as (S) are related to nonmoral sentences such as (T) in that they are completed by them. That is the fourth thing I take him to have in mind. These things want explanation.

Harman says:

> Motion is a relative matter. Motion is always relative to a choice of spatio-temporal framework. Something that is moving in relation to one spatio-temporal framework can be at rest in relation to another . . . [T]he only truth there is in this area is relative truth. (sec. 1.1)

Thus being in motion is not a one-place property; it is rather a two-place relation, between an entity X and a spatio-temporal framework S. So

(S′) Alfred is moving

is incomplete in that it contains only one referring expression ("Alfred"), and thus it has no truth-value. However certain sentences constructible from (S′) do have truth-values. Let us give spatio-temporal frameworks names: Stanley, Steven, and so on. Then

(T′) Alfred is moving relative to Stanley,

and

Alfred is moving relative to Steven,

and so on, are completions of (S′) and do have truth-values.

Harman also gives us a more abstruse example, namely mass. As Einstein has taught us, he says, "even an object's mass is relative to a choice of spatio-temporal framework" (sec. 1.1). Thus having a certain mass is not a two-place relation; it is rather a three-place relation, among an entity X, a measure M, and a spatio-temporal framework S. So sentences of the form "The mass of X is M" are also incomplete and thus lack truth-values; the relevant sentences of the form "The mass of X is M relative to S" are their completions and do have truth-values.

Yet another, simpler, example would have been relative height. Being taller is not a one-place property; it is rather a two-place relation, between a pair of entities X and Y. So "Alice is taller" is incomplete and thus lacks a truth-value; "Alice is taller than Jane" and "Alice is taller than Joan" are among its completions and do have truth-values.

Let us return to motion. Being in motion, Harman says, is a two-place relation between an entity X and a spatio-temporal framework S; since (S') contains only one referring expression ("Alfred"), (S') is incomplete. We are to agree that moral wrongness is a three-place relation among a moral framework M, a person P, and an act-kind D; since (S) contains only two referring expressions ("Paul" and "dancing"), (S) is incomplete. Therefore (S), like (S'), lacks a truth-value. Expressions like (T) are completions of (S) as expressions like (T') are completions of (S') and do have truth-values. And so similarly for moral sentences of other forms than (S).

In short, then, Moral Relativism says that moral sentences have no truth-values, and that is because they are incomplete; nonmoral sentences constructed in the way Harman indicated do have truth-values, and are completions of moral sentences.

Harman tells us that the Moral Relativist makes further claims, and I will draw attention to one of them later. Meanwhile, however, it is plain that if the Moral Relativist is right in saying that moral sentences have no truth-values, then it is not possible to find out about any moral sentences that they are true, and the thesis I called the Thesis of Moral Objectivity (in my Introduction to Part II) is false. Moral Relativism is therefore a direct threat to moral objectivity, and a friend of moral objectivity must find some way of responding to it.

10.2 Moral Relativists are not of course the only philosophers who believe that moral sentences have no truth- values: they share that idea with the Letter-Emotivists. We might well wonder, therefore, how Harman is to reply to the objections to that idea which I described in chapter 7, section 7.3. For example, I said that arguments such as the following are surely valid:

> If Paul's dancing offends people, then it would be morally wrong of Paul to engage in dancing,
> Paul's dancing offends people,
> Therefore, it would be morally wrong of Paul to engage in dancing.

But they cannot be, if moral sentences have no truth-values. Harman, I am sure, would reply that that argument is not valid, since its first premise and its conclusion lack truth-values – just as the following is not valid, and for the same reason:

> If Alfred is on the moon, then Alfred is moving.
> Alfred is on the moon,
> Therefore, Alfred is moving.

He could say that completions of these arguments are valid, however: for example, that

> If Paul's dancing offends people, then in relation to Mark, it would be morally wrong of Paul to engage in dancing,
> Paul's dancing offends people,
> Therefore, in relation to Mark, it would be morally wrong of Paul to engage in dancing,

is valid, just as is

> If Alfred is on the moon, then Alfred is moving relative to Stanley,
> Alfred is on the moon,
> Therefore, Alfred is moving relative to Stanley.

Harman might go on to say: "Were you struck by the fact that 'It would be morally wrong of Paul to engage in dancing' is a thoroughly respectable declarative sentence? And was it for *that* reason that you thought the first argument is valid? You shouldn't have drawn this conclusion from that premise, for 'Alfred is moving' is also a thoroughly respectable declarative sentence, and yet, since it lacks a truth-value, the second argument is not valid."[2]

And now isn't that an entirely adequate reply? Well, are moral sentences incomplete? I turn to that question in section 10.5 below. Let us first take note of an unclarity in what we have been told so far.

10.3 Our attention has been drawn to the fact that

(S') Alfred is moving

is incomplete; as Harman put it, "the only truth there is in this area is relative truth." By contrast,

(T') Alfred is moving relative to Stanley

has a truth-value, and might indeed be true. So similarly (we are to agree),

(S) It would be morally wrong of Paul to engage in dancing

lacks a truth-value, though by contrast,

(T) In relation to Mark, it would be morally wrong of Paul to engage in dancing

has a truth-value, and might indeed be true. But what does (T) *say*? We know what (T') says: it says that Alfred's spatial

[2] Harman might add: Was it also for that reason that you thought the result of inserting the sentence in the disquotation schema – namely " 'It would be morally wrong of Paul to engate in dancing' is true if and only if it would be morally wrong of Paul to engage in dancing" – had better be true? You shouldn't have drawn this conclusion from that premise, for " 'Alfred is moving' is true if and only if Alfred is moving" has no truth-value, and a fortiori is not true.

coordinates in Stanley are changing with change in his temporal coordinates in Stanley. What about (T)?

What in fact are those moral frameworks Mark, Matthew, Michael, and the rest? I said that Harman tells us that the Moral Relativist makes some further claims besides the ones I began with. Another is this:

> There is no single true morality. There are many different moral frameworks, none of which is more correct than the others. (sec. 1.2)

That suggests that a moral framework is itself a morality.

But what is a morality? You might think that a morality is something that a person might believe. That cannot be Harman's view, for on his view moral sentences have no truth-values, and there therefore are no moral beliefs.

Should we instead take a morality to be a set of (truth-value-less) moral sentences, which a person might (not believe, but) in some sense accept or assent to or endorse? And are we then to take (T) to say

> Mark has among its members the sentence (S)?

Or should we instead take a morality to be a set of attitudes (pro and con) which a person might have? And are we then to take (T) to say

> Mark has among its members a con-attitude toward Paul's dancing?

Or should we instead take a morality to be a set of entities of some other kind, and then take (T) to say that Mark has the appropriate one of them among its members?[3]

If we choose *any* of these options, a rather dramatic disanalogy emerges between moral rightness and wrongness on the one hand, and motion on the other hand. For whatever Stanley may be, (T') is contingent. Suppose Stanley is a spatio-temporal

---

[3] Wong (1984) says moralities are sets of rules. Harman himself says "By 'a moral system of coordinates' I mean a set of values (standards, principles, etc.)" (sec. 1.3), and I take it that moralities are moral systems of coordinates. Are values (standards, principles, etc.) sentences? Are they attitudes? Or are they entities of some other kind?

framework in which the earth is at rest. If Alfred is on the moon, then, since the moon's spatial coordinates in Stanley are changing with change in its temporal coordinates in Stanley, so are Alfred's. If Alfred had instead been on the earth, and indeed standing stock still on the earth, then it would not have been the case that Alfred's spatial coordinates in Stanley were changing with change in his temporal coordinates in Stanley, and thus it would not have been the case that Alfred was moving relative to Stanley.

If what (T) says is that Mark has (S) among its members, then (T) is not contingent, for if Mark has (S) among its members, then Mark would have had (S) among its members no matter what the world was like – for example, no matter what Paul's dancing would be like, no matter what effects it would have, no matter whether Paul had or had not promised not to dance, or anything else of the sort.

So also if Mark is not a set of sentences, but of attitudes. So also if Mark is a set of entities of any kind you like.[4]

Harman had said about motion that "the only truth there is in this area is relative truth," and invited us to say the same about moral rightness and wrongness. If moral frameworks are sets, and the results of prefixing a moral sentence by an expression of the form "In relation to moral framework M" say that the set M has such and such member, then the only truth in the area of moral rightness and wrongness – unlike that of motion – is necessary truth, and the only falsehood necessary falsehood.

Would Harman accept this disanalogy? He could, of course. He could say that he meant to draw our attention merely to an

---

[4] Harman wishes to allow that a person might be mistaken about what his own moral framework is (sec. 1.3). That is entirely compatible with moral frameworks' being sets, and with its therefore not being contingent that a particular moral framework does or does not have a particular member: anyone who likes this idea needs merely to suppose that a person might be mistaken about which of the moral frameworks – Mark, Matthew, and so on – is his own.

So also is the idea compatible with its being the case that (as we laymen would describe the situation) Paula believes it would be morally wrong for Paul to dance, but would not have believed this if she hadn't believed Paul promised not to dance: anyone who likes the idea needs merely to redescribe the situation in the words "Paula's moral framework contains X but she would instead have had a moral framework that does not contain X if she hadn't believed Paul promised not to dance," for suitable entity X.

analogy and not to an identity. Alternatively, he could say that moral frameworks are not after all sets. Or that while moral frameworks are sets, the results of prefixing a moral sentence by an expression of the form "In relation to moral framework M" do not say anything so simple as that the set M has such and such member. There are lots of possibilities. He doesn't tell us which he prefers.[5]

Let us in any case now bypass questions of detail and turn to the question whether we should accept the central idea of Harman's Moral Relativism, namely that moral sentences are incomplete.

10.4 Harman tells us that that Moral Relativism is "a reasonable inference from the most *plausible explanation* of the range of moral diversity that actually exists" (sec. 1.2). He says:

> One of the most important things to explain about moral diversity
> is that it occurs not just between societies but also within so-
> cieties and in a way that leads to seemingly intractable moral
> disagreements . . . [and these] differences often seem to rest on

[5] In fact the Moral Relativist must tell us more than merely what he has in mind by moral frameworks, and what is said by the likes of (T): he must also explain how an assertion of (T) turns out to be an attribution of the appropriate three-place relation to Mark, Paul, and dancing.

Moreover, he must tell us what in general marks a sentence as the completion of a moral sentence. Thus we took it for obvious that (T) completes (S) as (T') completes (S'). But what completes "It is not the case that it would be morally wrong of Paul to dance"? Let us abbreviate "in relation to M" as "M", and let "Q" be an abbreviation of any moral sentence. What is the completion of "-Q"? "M(-Q)"? or "-(MQ)"? (Or are these supposed to be equivalent? If they are to be, and moral frameworks are sets of moral sentences, then a completeness constraint needs to be imposed on moral frameworks: for every moral sentence, every moral framework needs to contain either it or its negation and not both.)

Again, why complete the first of the arguments I set out in section 10.2 in the way I did? Let "P" be an abbreviation of any contingent, nonmoral sentence. I completed the argument by taking its first premise to have the form "P→MQ"; why that rather than "M(P→Q)"? (If these are to be equivalent, then further, more complex completeness constraints need to be imposed on moral frameworks.)

And so on, for more complex examples.

I see no theoretical imposibility here, however; the question is only whether carrying out the (very messy) task required would repay its costs. (See footnote 4 to chapter 7, which cites analogous efforts by Letter-Emotivists to respond to Geach's objection.)

differences in basic values rather than on differences in circumstances or information.

He reminds us that we seem to have intractable moral disagreements about abortion and euthanasia, about whether it is morally
acceptable to raise animals for food, and so on. And he says:

> It is hard to see how to account for all moral disagreements in
> terms of differences in situation or beliefs about nonmoral facts.
> Many moral disagreements seem to rest instead on basic differen-
> ces in moral outlook.

He says that the most plausible explanation of the existence of
such disagreements is Moral Relativism: those disagreements
are like the "ancient" disagreement about whether the sun
moves or the earth moves (sec. 1.3).

How like that ancient disagreement? For a reason that will
emerge shortly, we need to be clear about this.

The sentences asserted by the parties to the ancient disagreement, namely

(1) The sun is moving

and

(1′) The earth is moving

have no truth-values. Consider the disagreement between those
who assert

(M) Permitting abortion is morally wrong

and those who assert

(M′) Permitting abortion is morally right.

According to Harman, (M) and (M′) are like (1) and (1′) in that
they too lack truth-values.

Now the fact (supposing it a fact) that (M) and (M′) are like (1) and (1′) in lacking truth-values would happily explain the seeming intractability of the disagreement between those who assert (M) and those who assert (M′). If what the parties assert have no truth-values, it would be no wonder that neither party has been able to convince the other of the truth of what he asserts.

But that (M) and (M′) are like (1) and (1′) in lacking truth-values cannot be the only likeness Harman has in mind between (M) and (M′) on the one hand, and (1) and (1′) on the other hand. Else he would have given us no reason to accept that Moral Relativism is the most plausible explanation of seeming intractability in moral disagreement.

For Moral Relativism is the most plausible explanation of seeming intractability in moral disagreement only if it is a more plausible explanation of that phenomenon than Letter-Emotivism is. But the Letter-Emotivist too believes that (M) and (M′) lack truth-values; thus he too believes that (M) and (M′) are like (1) and (1′) in lacking truth-values.

So Harman must have in mind a further likeness between (M) and (M′) on the one hand, and (1) and (1′) on the other hand. And indeed he does, and we know what it is. He thinks that (M) and (M′) are like (1) and (1′) in lacking truth-values because they are incomplete.

Not so, says the Letter-Emotivist. According to the Letter-Emotivist, (M) and (M′) *are* like (1) and (1′) in lacking truth-values, but they are unlike (1) and (1′) in what makes them lack truth-values. According to the Letter-Emotivist, (M) and (M′) do not lack truth-values because they are incomplete; they lack truth-values because – like

(2) Boo to broccoli!

and

(2′) Hooray to broccoli! –

assertions of them are mere displays of attitudes.

So Moral Relativism is the most plausible explanation of the existence of seeming intractability in moral disagreement only if the Moral Relativist's idea that moral sentences are incomplete is more plausible than the Letter-Emotivist's idea that assertions of moral sentences are mere displays of attitudes. Is it?[6]

We should be clear that the existence of seeming intractability in moral disagreement does not by itself select between these ideas. Both ideas yield that (M) and (M') lack truth-values, and therefore both would happily explain the seeming intractability of the disagreement between those who assert (M) and those who assert (M'), for as I said, if what the parties to that disagreement assert have no truth-values, it would be no wonder that neither party has been able to convince the other of the truth of what he asserts.

10.5 Does Harman have reason to believe that his idea is more plausible than the Letter-Emotivist's?

Consider Paula again. I invited you to suppose she asserted

(S) It would be morally wrong of Paul to engage in dancing.

According to the Letter-Emotivist, assertions of moral sentences are mere displays of attitudes: the speech-act the speaker performs is the same as the speech-act he would have performed if he had instead asserted the relevant expression of the

---

[6] Harman had discussed this question briefly, but inconclusively, in Harman (1991). The question does not reappear in his contribution to this volume.

A reminder is in order that Moral Relativism is the most plausible explanation of seeming intractability in moral disagreement only if the moral relativist's idea that moral sentences are incomplete is *also* more plausible than the subjectivist's idea that moral sentences are like

    (3) I dislike broccoli

and

    (3') I like broccoli

in containing (as part of their meanings) a first-person singular pronoun. Neither Harman nor I have discussed subjectivism, since hardly anybody nowadays thinks it plausible. But there are ways of updating the intuition that lies behind it. James Dreier calls the theory he presents in Dreier (1990) "Speaker Relativism"; in light of its claiming that a speaker's own moral framework is what matters, his theory seems to me to be better viewed, not as a version of relativism, but instead as a sophisticated version of subjectivism.

form "Boo to . . . !" or "Hooray to . . . !" In particular, when Paula
asserted (S), she merely displayed an attitude: the speech-act she
performed is the same as the speech-act she would have been
performing had she instead asserted "Boo to Paul's dancing!"

What, on Harman's view, is the speech-act performed by one
who asserts a moral sentence? What was Paula doing in asserting (S)?

I said that it might have been moral framework Mark that was
conspicuous to Paula at the time of asserting (S). I did not invite
you to suppose that Mark is her own moral framework, or for
that matter that it is not. Let us now suppose that Mark is
Paula's own moral framework. Then I am sure Harman would
say she displayed a con-attitude toward Paul's dancing in asserting (S).[7] I am sure he would say, more strongly, that she
merely displayed a con-attitude toward Paul's dancing in asserting (S). After all, on his view, like that of the Letter-Emotivist, (S) has no truth-value, and he had told us we are not to
suppose him to be claiming that Paula meant or intended to be
asserting anything about Mark *by* asserting (S): on Harman's
view, Paula meant no more than she said, and what she said
was only (S).

Does Harman believe that (i) whenever people assert moral
sentences it is always their own moral frameworks that are
conspicuous to them? Suppose he does. Then he is committed
to thinking it true quite generally that assertions of moral sentences are mere displays of attitudes. But that is the Letter-
Emotivist's idea. Harman therefore cannot say that his own idea
that moral sentences are incomplete is more plausible than the
Letter-Emotivist's idea that assertions of moral sentences are
mere displays of attitudes.

Perhaps Harman would back down: that is, perhaps he would
say that the two ideas are equally plausible. (Thus perhaps he

---

[7] Harman draws our attention to what he calls "the quasi-absolutist use of
moral terminology" in chapter 3, section 3.2.; if I have understood him, he
would say that you use the term "wrong" quasi-absolutistically just in case it is
your own moral framework that is conspicuous to you at the time of using it.
He then goes on to say that when you use "wrong" in that way, you are
"expressing" your attitude toward certain standards, and he adds that expressing an attitude is not saying you have it.

would opt for Letter-Emotivism as well as for Moral Relativism.) But what reason does he have for thinking that moral sentences are incomplete, given he accepts the Letter-Emotivist's idea that assertions of them are mere displays of attitudes? (Thus what reason does he have for opting for Moral Relativism as well as for Letter-Emotivism?)

Let us go back. Being in motion, Harman said, is a two-place relation between an entity X and a spatio-temporal framework S; it follows that

(S′) Alfred is moving

is incomplete in that it contains only one referring expression ("Alfred") –

(T′) Alfred is moving relative to Stanley

is among its completions. We were to agree that moral wrongness is a three-place relation among moral framework M, a person P, and an act-kind D; if we agree to this then we are agreeing that (S) is incomplete in that it contains only two referring expressions ("Paul" and "dancing") –

(T) In relation to Mark, it would be morally wrong of Paul to engage in dancing

is among its completions. But if you accept the Letter- Emotivist's idea that assertions of moral sentences are mere displays of attitudes, what reason could you have for thinking that moral wrongness is a three-place relation? From his idea, the Letter-Emotivist draws the conclusion that there is no such property or relation as moral wrongness; if you accept his idea, that seems to be exactly the conclusion you should draw.

The Letter-Emotivist thinks that sentences like (T) do predicate a three-place relation. Perhaps he would say that (T) says

(T*) Mark contains a con-attitude toward Paul's engaging in dancing.

But he would insist that the three-place relation predicated by (T*), and thus by (T), is not moral wrongness, since there isn't any such property or relation as moral wrongness. And he would add the following. While a variety of expressions are completed by (T*), (S) is not among them. For example, the expression

contains a con-attitude toward Paul's engaging in dancing

is incomplete, and (T*) is among its completions. The expression

Mark contains a con-attitude toward Paul's engaging in

is also incomplete; (T*) is among its completions too. But (T*) no more completes (S) than it completes "Boo to Paul's dancing!". More strongly, nothing completes (S) just as nothing completes "Boo to Paul's dancing!": neither is incomplete.

In sum, the Letter-Emotivist draws three conclusions from his idea that assertions of moral sentences are mere displays of attitudes. *First*, that there is no such relation as moral wrongness, and hence (T) does not predicate moral wrongness. *Second*, (T*) does not complete (S), and thus (T) does not complete (S). *Third*, nothing completes (S): (S) is not incomplete.

Harman might argue that those three things do not follow from the Letter-Emotivist's idea that assertions of moral sentences are mere displays of attitudes. (It is hard to see how he is to do this, however.) Alternatively, and I suspect more likely, he might simply reject the idea.

For he might reject the supposition I made just above: that is, he might deny that (i) whenever people assert moral sentences it is always their own moral frameworks that are conspicuous to them. He might say instead that (ii) some people sometimes assert moral sentences when it is not their own moral frameworks that are conspicuous to them. That is in any case what his paradigm encourages us to take him to have in mind. Sometimes when Alice asserts (S′), the spatio-temporal framework that is conspicuous to her is a spatio-temporal framework in

which she is at rest, but sometimes the spatio-temporal framework that is conspicuous to her is one in which she is not at
rest; so we might well have supposed Harman to have in mind,
by analogy, that while sometimes when Paula asserts (S), the
moral framework that is conspicuous to her is her own moral
framework, sometimes the moral framework that is conspicuous to her is someone else's.

And if he does say (ii), he is not committed to accepting the
Letter-Emotivist's idea that assertions of moral sentences are
mere displays of attitudes. Quite to the contrary. For suppose it
was Matthew that was conspicuous to Paula at the time of
asserting (S), and that Matthew is not Paula's own moral framework. Then Paula was not displaying any attitude of her own,
either pro or con, toward Paul's dancing. It follows that the
thesis that assertions of moral sentences are mere displays of
attitudes is false: for here is Paula, who was not displaying an
attitude in asserting (S), and who, a fortiori, was not merely
displaying an attitude in asserting (S).

It is a good question how Harman is to get from (ii) to his own
claims, namely that the three-place relation predicated by (T) is
moral wrongness, and that (T) is a completion of (S). But let us
bypass it. For the prior question is whether (ii) can be right. *Do
people ever assert moral sentences when it is not their own
moral frameworks that are conspicuous to them?* I find it very
hard to imagine circumstances in which a person might do this,
and Harman does not himself describe any.

Perhaps an anthropologist has been living with the Anti-
Dancers, a small tribe in the North-west. She returns and gives
a report on her stay with them. I come in in the middle of her
talk and hear her say

(S+) It would be morally wrong of anyone to engage in
      dancing.

I am surprised, and ask her later whether she really thinks so.
"No of course I don't," she snaps; "it's their morality I was
reporting on." So perhaps people do sometimes assert moral
sentences when it is someone else's moral framework that is
conspicuous to them.

This won't do at all, however. The anthropologist did not assert (S+). She uttered it, of course, but only as part of her report on the tribe's morality; that is, (S+) fell within the scope of the prefix "On moral matters, the Anti-Dancers believe". She no more asserted (S+) in the part of her talk that I heard than she asserted

(S@) Rain is a gift from the Rain God, who lives on the moon

in the earlier part of her talk that I missed. She uttered (S@) then, but only as part of her report on the tribe's cosmology; that is, (S@) fell within the scope of the prefix "On cosmological matters, the Anti-Dancers believe". And a defense of the idea that sentences of the form " . . . is morally wrong" are incomplete that rests on her uttering (S+) when it was not her own moral framework that was conspicuous to her would be no stronger than a defense of the (thoroughly weird!) idea that sentences of the form "Rain is . . . " are incomplete that rests on her uttering (S@) when it was not her own cosmological framework that was conspicuous to her.

In short, it seems to me plain that no one asserts – should we say no one *seriously* asserts? – a moral sentence when it is someone else's moral framework that is conspicuous to him. If that is right, then so far as I can see, Harman has no reason to believe that moral sentences are incomplete.

We should notice also that if moral sentences are not incomplete, then the objection to the thesis that moral sentences lack truth-values that I reminded you of in section 10.2 above cannot be responded to in the way I said Harman would respond to it. Thus it cannot be said that the first of the arguments I drew attention to there is invalid in the same way as, and for the same reason as, the second of them is invalid.[8] So the objection remains.

10.6 How is the existence of seemingly intractable moral disagreement to be explained? I have suggested that Moral Relativism is not a more plausible explanation than Letter-Emotivism.

---

[8] Nor can he make the response to the objection from 'disquotation' that I drew attention to the possibility of in footnote 2 above.

But I believe that Letter-Emotivism is not at all plausible; I drew attention to objections to Letter-Emotivism in chapter 7.

My own view is that the most plausible explanation of the existence of one such disagreement may perfectly well differ from that of another.

In some cases, the source of the apparent intractability is the fact that the issues in dispute are just plain hard, hard in that deciding what to think about them has implications for a wide variety of kinds of action. Abortion, euthanasia: coming to a view about them has a bearing on what we should think about taking life and allowing death quite generally, about the limits to freedom, about the duties we do or do not have to others, and so on and on. We can think of conclusions about those issues as relatively central to the moral network: replace one conclusion with another and the entire network must change in shape.

In other cases, the source of the trouble is what I have elsewhere called walling off. We may have good reason to think that one party is ignoring what he knows to be the case, or failing to take it seriously. Or he may be failing to connect one belief with another. I think "walling off" a good general description of this kind of phenomenon – people are the more prone to engage in it the more it profits them to protect a moral belief from threats to it.[9] We should keep in mind, moreover, that walling off is entirely familiar in argument about nonmoral issues too: people are quite generally prone to protecting beliefs they have made investments in.

It is a gross oversimplication of moral disagreement to think it undecidable unless it issues from "differences in situation or beliefs about nonmoral facts," as Harman put it.

There remains a possibility that some seemingly intractable moral disagreement is due to indeterminacy, there just being no

[9] There is strong pressure in most of us to protect a moral belief to the effect that our own conduct is morally acceptable. (That shows something good as well as something bad in us.) Among Harman's examples of practices about which societies differ was slavery, so it pays to take note of the fact that walling off was very common among American slave-owners, and not surprisingly. James Oakes reports that when asked his views about slavery, "George Washington admitted, 'I shall frankly declare to you that I do not like even to think, much less talk, of it.' " (Oakes, 1983, p. 120.) [My earlier discussion of walling off appears in Thomson (1990).]

answer to the question which party is right. It pays to stress, however, that there being no answer to a hard moral question (if there is no answer to it) does not show anything about simpler moral questions. In particular, accommodating moral indeterminacy (if we must) does not require or even lend weight to the idea that all moral thought is mere sea of attitudes.

10.7 I began section 10.1 by quoting one of Harman's theses, and I mentioned, parenthetically, that he says it is merely "a first approximation" to the thesis he means to advance. He invites us to accept a revision in his section 3.4. I am sorry that I cannot responsibly comment on the revision since I am not sure that I have understood the machinery he makes use of in it.

The machinery gets introduced in section 3.2, where he draws our attention to what he calls "the quasi-absolutist use of moral terminology". If I have understood him, what he means is that you use a moral term quasi-absolutistically just in case it is your own moral framework that is conspicuous to you at the time of using it. He invites us to use capital letters "to mark" that use of moral terminology: we are to make use of the expression "WRONG" to mark that use of "morally wrong." (And later we are also to make use of the expressions "UNREASONABLE," "REASONS," and "JUSTIFICATION" for a similar purpose.) Harman does not help us much to be clear about the meaning of "WRONG", but if I have understood him, what he has in mind is this. If a person asserts "Such and such is morally wrong" then if (and only if) it was his own moral framework that was conspicuous to him at the time, he could as well have asserted, instead, "Such and such is WRONG." Moreover, if a person asserts "Such and such is morally wrong" then if (and only if) it was his own moral framework that was conspicuous to him at the time, *we* can correctly say about him "He said that such and such is WRONG."

Thus consider Paula, who asserted "It would be morally wrong of Paul to engage in dancing." Suppose (i) that it was her own moral framework that was conspicuous to her at the time. Then she was using "wrong" quasi-absolutistically. So she could as well have asserted, instead, "It would be WRONG of Paul to engage in dancing," and we can correctly say about her "She said that it would be WRONG of Paul to engage in dancing". Suppose (ii) that it was not her own moral framework that was conspicuous to her at the time. Then she was not using "wrong" quasi-absolutistically. So she could not as well have asserted, instead, "It would be WRONG of Paul to engage in dancing", and we cannot correctly say about her "She said that it would be WRONG of Paul to engage in dancing."

Now I suggested in section 10.5 that it is always our own moral framework that is conspicuous to us when we assert moral sentences, so if that is what Harman has in mind, then it seems to me that our (serious assertive) use of moral terms is always quasi-absolutist. *Everyone* who asserts "Such and such is morally wrong" says that the such and such would be WRONG. Hence the new expression "WRONG" is otiose: it answers to no distinction.

But I may have misunderstood Harman. For shortly after telling us that these capitalized expressions are intended "to mark the quasi-absolutist *use* of moral terminology" (my italics), he says what makes it appear that "is WRONG" is a predicate, indeed, a predicate with a hidden first-person singular pronoun. He says: "a moral relativist who also uses QA [quasi-absolutist] terminology" should accept

X is WRONG if and only if X is wrong in relation to the morality relevantly associated with my current values. (sec. 3.2)

This suggests that if Paula asserts "Paul's dancing is WRONG," then she thereby asserts something true just in case Paul's dancing is wrong in relation to Paula's own moral framework – and this no matter what moral framework was conspicuous to her at the time of asserting "Paul's dancing is wrong."[10] (It might be worth mentioning that expressions of the form "X is WRONG," so understood, are not incomplete. They are analogous, not to

---

[10] Alternatively put: if Paula asserts the *sentence* "Paul's dancing is WRONG," then she thereby asserts the *proposition* that Paul's dancing is wrong in relation to Paula's own moral framework.

"Alfred is moving," but rather to "Alfred is moving relative to a spatio-temporal framework in which I am at rest."[11])

I must therefore bypass the revision of Harman's thesis that he invites us to accept in section 3.4.

10.8 I said I would have space to comment on only two of the theses Harman advances, but the second of the two is not strictly speaking a thesis he *advances*. He invites us to attend to it, and he appears to think it true, but he does not explicitly tell us that we are to think it true.

Harman expresses the thesis as follows: "when a moral requirement applies to someone, that person has compelling reasons to do what he or she is required to do" (opening of chapter 4). Let us take Alice to be our representative person, and dancing to be our representative act-kind. Then the thesis says:

> Morality requires Alice to dance only if Alice has compelling reasons to dance.

What is it to have compelling reasons to do a thing? Harman defines that phrase as follows: a person has compelling reasons to do a thing if and only if all things considered, it would be reasonable for the person to do the thing and it would not be reasonable for the person not to do it. He also uses the terms "rational" and "irrational" in this connection, and I am sure he would say that the following comes to the same: a person has compelling reasons to do a thing if and only if all things considered, it would be rational for the person to do the thing and irrational for the person not to do the thing. Thus the words I used to express the thesis mean the following:

> Morality requires Alice to dance only if all things considered, it would be rational for Alice to dance and irrational for her not to dance.

---

[11] So if we interpret Harman's "WRONG" in this way, we are taking him to be a subjectivist about the predicate "is WRONG." See footnote 6 above.

That supplies us with a necessary condition for moral require-ment; under what conditions does that necessary condition fail to be met? That is, under what conditions is

(1) All things considered, it would be rational for Alice to dance and irrational for her not to dance

false? Harman is unfortunately not explicit about this matter, and there are a number of possible interpretations of what he has in mind. One way of interpreting him is this. Suppose Alice has no wants that would be met by dancing and has wants that would be met by not dancing. And suppose that her being in that mental state is not due to an epistemic failure. (Suppose, that is, that her being in that mental state is not due to nonmoral ignorance, failure to reason correctly, and so on.) Suppose, that is, that

(2) Alice has no wants that would be met by dancing and has wants that would be met by not dancing, and her being in that mental state is not due to an epistemic failure

is true. We can, and I will, take Harman to think that if (2) is true, then (1) is false.[12]

What we have reached, then, is this. Suppose (2) is true. It follows that (1) is false. It follows that morality does not require Alice to dance.

Dancing being merely our representative act-kind, we have reached the following quite general thesis:

Agent Relativism: If Alice has no wants that would be met by doing such and such and has wants that would be met by not doing it, and if, also, her being in that mental state is not due to an epistemic failure, then morality does not require her to do the such and such.

---

[12] What I point to by the expression "epistemic failure" was suggested by the following passage in Harman's text: "It is easy to think of [successful happy

(I will explain my reason for choosing that name for the thesis shortly.)

Before turning to the question what we should think of this thesis, we should ask: can *Harman* consistently believe Agent Relativism is true? Harman, as he told us, is a Moral Relativist: on his view,

> Morality requires Alice to dance

has no truth-value. A fortiori, so also does its negation, namely

(3) It is not the case that morality requires Alice to dance,

have no truth-value. How, then, can he be inviting us to take seriously that (3) is true if (2) is true?

Many people distinguish among varieties of relativism. Following Harman, I called the thesis we looked at in earlier sections "Moral Relativism"; many people would prefer to call it a version of "appraiser relativism", since it addresses itself to what is said by an appraiser. Harman himself suggests "critic relativism," and let us follow him: I will from here on call the thesis we looked at in earlier sections "Critic Relativism".

---

criminals] who lack motivation to observe basic moral requirements, and not because of any nonmoral ignorance on their part, any failure to reason correctly, any weakness of will, or any other sort of failure to appreciate reasons to observe the requirement in question. It is difficult to see how such people could nevertheless have compelling reason to observe the moral requirements" (sec. 4.2).

Another way of interpreting Harman is this: if

(2') Alice's moral framework does not contain 'Morality requires Alice to dance'

is true, then (1) is false. Yet another is this: if

(2") Alice has no wants that would be met by dancing and has wants that would be met by not dancing, and her being in that mental state is not due to an epistemic failure, *and* Alice's moral framework does not contain 'Morality requires Alice to dance'

is true, then (1) is false. Or would he say that (2) entails (2') and (2"), so that whatever they are sufficient for, (2) is itself sufficient for? In any case, the objections I will make to the idea that if (2) is true, then Alice need not dance, could easily be revised so as to count equally against the ideas that if (2') or (2") is true, then Alice need not dance.

The thesis we are now looking at is commonly called a version of "agent relativism," since it addresses itself to features of an agent being appraised. Hence my choice of name for the thesis.

And now: what is the relation between Critic Relativism and Agent Relativism? The answer is that they are at war with each other.[13] To believe Critic Relativism is true is to be committed to the idea that (3) has no truth-value; to believe Agent Relativism is true is to be committed to the idea that (3) is true if (2) is true. So if you believe that the likes of (2) are sometimes true, you cannot consistently also believe that both Critic Relativism and Agent Relativism are true.

Harman is certainly a Critic Relativist, and presumably therefore does not believe Agent Relativism is true. Presumably it was his commitment to Critic Relativism that explains why he did not strictly speaking *advance* the thesis I am calling Agent Relativism, but merely set it before us. Perhaps he merely intended to be setting before us something (truth-value-less) that is in his own moral framework, and inviting us to adopt a moral framework that contains it if ours does not already contain it. No matter. Agent Relativism is a thesis that many people have worried about, and we should have a closer look at it.

10.9 It is a good heuristic in philosophy to be suspicious of views that would shock your grocer. I order a bushel of apples from my grocer and he sends them round straightway. The following week he sends round his bill. I phone and say "Something interesting has happened. I now find that my wants have changed: I now find that I have no wants that would be met by paying your bill, and that I have wants that would be met by not paying your bill." (Or perhaps I say "If truth be told, what I wanted all along was just a bushel of free apples.") "Moreover," I go on, "my mental state is not due to any epistemic failure, for I have gone into this matter very carefully." I explain: "After all, you haven't any proof that you delivered the apples, and even if you did, there's nothing you could do about the matter since I'm leaving for Bolivia in the morning." And I go on: "So it

---

[13] A good discussion of the relations among several varieties of relativism is Lyons (1976).

follows that morality doesn't require me to pay you." I am sure
my grocer would regard this as outrageous. He'd say that if I
don't pay the bill I'm a rotten thief!

Let us take this slowly. The Agent Relativist says that my little
argument really was valid. He says that the premise

> (P) JT has no wants that would be met by paying the bill and
> has wants that would be met by not paying the bill, and
> JT's being in that mental state is not due to an epistemic
> failure

really does entail the conclusion

> (C) Morality does not require JT to pay the bill.

But how *can* the Agent Relativist think that (P) entails (C)? The
idea looks crazy. Surely it can't at all plausibly be thought that
I am relieved of a moral requirement whenever it so happens
that I have no wants that would be met by abiding by it, and
have wants that would be met by not abiding by it, and my
mental state is not due to an epistemic failure.

"Well," says the Agent Relativist, "if you look at the route by
which I recommend getting from the likes of (P) to the likes of
(C), you'll see that the idea isn't crazy at all." He says: "from (P)
there follows an intermediate conclusion, namely

> (IC) All things considered, it would be irrational for JT to
> pay the bill.

How so? On some views, an act's being rational just is its
efficiently satisfying the agent's wants, whatever those wants
may be. On other, probably sounder, views, an act's being
rational is its efficiently satisfying the agent's wants on condition that those wants are not due to epistemic failure. We
needn't decide which is sounder, for given (P), JT's not paying
the bill would efficiently satisfy her wants, *and* her wants are
not due to epistemic failure. So her not paying the bill would be
rational, and her paying the bill would be irrational." He goes
on: "and from (IC), (C) follows straightaway, for morality can't

be thought to require a person to do a thing if it would be irrational for the person to do it." He summarizes: "so (P) entails the intermediate conclusion (IC), and (IC) entails (C)." He concludes: "therefore despite appearances, (P) really does entail (C)."[14]

It is an interesting question why so many people who did or would have rejected the idea that (P) entails (C) are moved to accept it when they see the Agent Relativist's route from (P) to (C). When we think the idea that a certain premise entails a certain conclusion is crazy, we may turn out to be mistaken. Sometimes the route from a premise to a conclusion is very complex, tricky, and long, as it often is where what is in question is proving a theorem from a set of axioms. In such cases, supplying us with the route may surprise us, may convince us that yes, after all, the premise does entail the conclusion. But there is no complexity or trickiness in the Agent Relativist's route from (P) to (C); his route from (P) to (C) is in fact very short, for there is only one intermediate stop along the way, namely (IC). How could the apparent craziness of the trip from (P) to (C) be eliminated by stopping once along the way at (IC) as the Agent Relativist does?

The answer is that it can't be and isn't. Even those who are moved to agree with the Agent Relativist that (P) entails (C) – after the Agent Relativist shows them how to get from (P) to (C) – even *they* do not regard the idea that (P) entails (C) as itself plausible. That is because it isn't.

Let us look again at the first part of the Agent Relativist's route from (P) to (C), namely the part from (P) to (IC). That does seem acceptable: we are inclined to think (at worst we are easily persuaded to think) that the conception of rationality the Agent Relativist helps himself to is very plausible, perhaps even obvious. What else is there to an act's being rational than just its

---

[14] A shorter route from (P) to (C) goes as follows. "If (P) is true, then it would be pointless to say to JT that morality requires her to pay the bill, for given (P), JT isn't going to pay it. Therefore morality does not require JT to pay the bill." We should be clear that this is a bad argument. The fact that it would be pointless to say to JT that morality requires her to pay the bill is entirely compatible with its being true that morality requires her to do so. That this is a bad argument was drawn attention to by David Lyons in Lyons (1976).

efficiently satisfying the agent's wants, or anyway, its efficiently satisfying the agent's wants on condition that those wants are
not due to epistemic failure? Some people argue that that conception of rationality is too narrow and hence is mistaken.[15] If
they are right, the first part of the Agent Relativist's route is
blocked: he cannot get from (P) to (IC). But let us bypass the
question whether they are right. Let us ask: supposing that
conception of rationality is correct, and that the Agent Relativist therefore can get from (P) to (IC), what *then*?

The second part of the Agent Relativist's route from (P) to (C),
namely the part from (IC) to (C), also seems acceptable: we are
inclined to think that morality requires of a person only what it
would be rational for the person to do. But are we inclined to
think this while we have in mind a conception of rationality
according to which rationality in action just is an action's
efficiently satisfying the agent's wants, or anyway, its efficiently satisfying the agent's wants on condition that those wants are
not due to epistemic failure? I hardly think so. If we did, we
would regard it as obvious that (P) entails (C), and we don't.
Quite to the contrary.

It is not at all clear what conception of rationality we have in
mind when we think that morality requires of a person only
what it would be rational for the person to do. As I said, some
people have a particular, enlarged conception of rationality in
mind. Others probably have no conception of rationality in
mind at all. Perhaps they have in mind merely that morality
requires no more of one person than it requires of others.
Perhaps they have in mind merely that morality does not require a person to do a thing unless there are facts that are reason
for believing – in the sense of lending weight to the belief – that
morality requires the person to do the such and such. There are
other possibilities too. What is clear is only that we do not have
in mind a conception of rationality according to which rationality in action is a function of the agent's wants.

If we cannot seriously entertain both ideas at once – the idea
that rationality in action is a function of the agent's wants, and

---

[15] See, for example, Darwall (1983); Darwall also provides helpful discussion
of other efforts to enlarge the notion 'rationality.'

the idea that morality requires only what is rational – then a ground for rejecting the Agent Relativist's route from (P) to (C) suggests itself. We can say that in order to get from (P) to (C) by the route the Agent Relativist recommends, we have to change trains in mid-trip, and indeed, forget the train we took first while boarding the second. Thus we can say that while a certain conception of rationality gets us from (P) to (IC), we can go on from (IC) to (C) only if we forget that we got to (IC) from (P).

We would have a stronger ground for rejecting the Agent Relativist's route from (P) to (C) if we could say: not merely can we not seriously entertain both of those thoughts at once, but given the first is true, the second is false. It seems to me that there is conclusive reason for believing that that is exactly what we should say.

For let us go back to my grocer. I imagined myself drawing to his attention facts that make (P) true. I then imagined myself inviting him to agree that it follows that (C) is also true. Then I said to you: I am sure my grocer would regard this as outrageous. I said to you: he'd say that if I don't pay the bill I'm a rotten thief. Wouldn't he be *right* to say this?

Suppose (i) that he would be. Then

(Q) If JT does not pay the bill she's a rotten thief

is true. But that can't be true unless morality requires JT to pay the bill. (You don't earn the title "rotten thief" unless you fail to do what morality requires.) Alternatively put: if (Q) is true, then morality requires JT to pay the bill.

There is a more general point in the offing here. Being a rotten thief is only one of the many ways of being unjust, and if (Q) is true, so is

(Q*) JT's not paying the bill would be unjust.

The more general point is that if (Q*) is true, then morality requires JT to pay the bill.

The still more general point is that if a person, any person, would be acting unjustly in refraining from doing a thing, then it follows that morality requires the person to do the thing. This is an idea I drew attention to in chapter 8, section 8.10, and I hope it seemed not merely plausible but obvious. When once we have found out that a person would be acting unjustly in refraining from doing a thing, then there is nothing further that needs to be established before we are entitled to conclude that morality requires the person to do the thing.[16]

To return to our supposition, then. We are supposing (i) that my grocer would be right to say JT will be a rotten thief if she doesn't pay the bill. It follows that morality requires her to pay it. No matter that (P) is true: given (Q) is true, (C) is false.

Indeed, (C) is false even if the Agent Relativist's conception of rationality is correct, and thus even if (IC) follows from (P). No matter that (IC) is true as well as (P): given (Q) is true, (C) is false.

Thus (P) does not entail (C). Therefore if the idea that rationality in action is a function of the agent's wants is correct, then the idea that morality requires only what is rational is incorrect.

---

[16] Philippa Foot says in Foot (1978e): "moral epithets such as 'dishonest', 'unjust', 'uncharitable' . . . do not cease to apply to a man because he is indifferent to the ends of morality" (p. 172), and I am sure she would agree that JT's not paying the bill would be unjust, whatever JT's wants may be. Would she allow us to conclude that morality requires JT to pay the bill? Some of her remarks suggest that she would not. Thus, for example, she says she is

> putting forward quite seriously a theory that disallows that possibility of saying that a man ought (free unsubscripted 'ought') to have ends other than those he does have e.g. that the uncaring, amoral man ought to care about the relief of suffering or the protection of the weak. In my view we must start from the fact that some people do care about such things, and even devote their lives to them; they may therefore talk about what should be done presupposing such common aims. These things are necessary, but only subjectively and conditionally necessary, as Kant would put it (p. 170).

This passage suggests she would say that though JT's not paying the bill would be unjust, morality does not require JT to pay it.

On the other hand, it is not clear what she has in mind by the phrase "free unsubscripted 'ought'"; and it may be that she would say both that JT's not paying the bill would be unjust and that morality requires JT to pay it, and that she would deny only "JT ought (free unsubscripted 'ought') to pay it," where *that* would be true only if JT had reason to pay it. This second interpretation is suggested by the following, from Foot (1978b): "If a categorical imperative is understood as one that any man must automatically have reason to obey, then moral judgements are in my opinion not categorical imperatives" (p. xiii). For this passage suggests that moral judgments – such as "Morality requires JT to pay the bill" as well as "JT's not paying the bill would be unjust" – can be true even if JT has no reason to pay the bill.

There is logical space for rejecting the supposition (i) that my grocer would be right to say JT will be a rotten thief if she doesn't pay the bill. We could instead suppose (ii) that my grocer would be wrong to say this, and thus that (Q) is false. If we take this line we had better suppose that (Q*) is also false, since the truth of (Q*) also suffices to make (C) false. I say there is logical space for this idea, but it won't do at all. For what could be thought to make (Q*) false? By hypothesis, JT has no wants that would be met by paying the bill and has wants that would be met by not paying the bill, and JT's being in that mental state is not due to an epistemic failure. It would be absurd to conclude from this that her not paying the bill is after all not unjust. Perhaps the Agent Relativist's conception of rationality is correct, so that it follows from that fact about JT's wants that her paying the bill would be irrational. It would be no less absurd to conclude from *this* that her not paying the bill is after all not unjust. A person's own wants are always relevant to the question whether his or her doing a thing is unjust, but they never settle the matter, for the wants of others are always relevant too.

In sum, (P) is true in the story I told, but (C) is false. It is therefore neither here nor there whether the Agent Relativist can get from (P) to (IC); even if he can, he can't get from there to (C).

10.10 I have thought it best to focus in this reply on the two versions of relativism that Harman draws our attention to, since they are particularly important to him, and they have been found attractive by others as well. Moreover, the first of them is a direct threat to moral objectivity, which I have been concerned to defend throughout. But this means that I have been unable to discuss any of the other suggestions Harman makes along the way, and I regret this, since many of them seem to me not merely plausible but very much worth closer study.

Bibliography

Aquinas, T. (1256–9). St. Thomas Aquinas, *Truth*, Indianapolis/Cambridge: Hackett (1994).

Ayer, A. J. (1946). *Language, Truth and Logic*, 2nd edn, London: Victor Gollancz.

Beyleveld, D. (1991). *The Dialectical Necessity of Morality: An Analysis and Defense of Alan Gewirth's Argument to the Principle of Generic Consistency*, Chicago: Chicago University Press.

Blackburn, S. (1984). *Spreading the Word*, New York: Oxford University Press.

Blackburn, S. (1990). "Just causes," *Philosophical Studies*, reprinted in Blackburn (1993a).

Blackburn, S. (1993a). *Essays in Quasi-Realism*, Oxford: Oxford University Press.

Blackburn, S. (1993b). "The land of lost content," in R. G. Frey and C. W. Morris, *Value, Welfare, and Morality*, Cambridge: Cambridge University Press.

Brink, D. O. (1989). *Moral Realism and the Foundations of Ethics*, Cambridge: Cambridge University Press.

Burge, C. T. (1986). "Individualism and psychology." *Philosophical Review* **95**: 3–46.

Carey, S. (1990). "Cognitive development," in Daniel N. Osherson and Edward E. Smith (eds), *Thinking: An Invitation to Cognitive Science, Volume 3*, Cambridge, Mass.: MIT, pp. 146–72.

Daniels, N. O. (1985). *Just Health Care*, Cambridge: Cambridge University Press.

Darley, J. and Shultz, T. R. (1990). "Moral rules: their content and acquisition," *Annual Review of Psychology* **41**: 525–56.

Darwall, S., (1983). *Impartial Reason*. Ithaca, N.Y.: Cornell University Press.

Dreier, J. (1990). "Internalism and speaker relativism," *Ethics* **101**: 6–26.

Dworkin, R. (1986). *Law's Empire.* Cambridge, Mass.: Harvard University Press.

Dworkin, R. (1993). *Life's Dominion*, New York: Knopf.

Foot, P. (1978a). *Virtues and Vices and Other Essays in Moral Philosophy*, Oxford: Basil Blackwell.

Foot, P. (1978b). Introduction to Foot (1978a).

Foot, P. (1978c). "Virtues and vices," in Foot (1978a).

Foot, P. (1978d). "The problem of abortion and the doctrine of the double effect," reprinted in Foot (1978a).

Foot, P. (1978e). "Morality as a system of hypothetical imperatives," reprinted (with revisions) in Foot (1978a).

Foot, P. (1985). "Utilitarianism and the virtues," *Mind* **94**, reprinted in Samuel Scheffler, *Consequentialism and its Critics*, Oxford: Oxford University Press, 1988.

Flanagan, O. (1991). *Varieties of Moral Personality*, Cambridge, Mass.: Harvard University Press.

Gauthier, D. (1986). *Morals by Agreement.* Oxford: Oxford University Press.

Geach, P. (1965). "Assertion," *Philosophical Review* **74**.

Gewirth, D. (1977). *Reason and Morality* Chicago: Chicago University Press.

Gibbard, A. (1990). *Wise Choices, Apt Feelings*, Cambridge, Mass.: Harvard University Press.

Gibbard, A. (1993). "Reply to Sinnott–Armstrong," *Philosophical Studies* **69**.

Gilbert, M. (1989). *On Social Facts*, London: Routledge.

Gilligan, C. (1982). *In a Different Voice: Psychological Theory and Women's Development* Cambridge, Mass.: Harvard University Press.

Goodman, N. (1965). *Fact, Fiction, and Forecast.* Cambridge, Mass.: Harvard University Press.

Hamilton, W. D. (1964). "The genetic evolution of social behavior," *Journal of Theoretical Biology* **7**: 1–16.

Hardin, R. (1988). *Morality within the Limits of Reason.* Chicago: University of Chicago Press.

Hare, R. M. (1952). *The Language of Morals*, Oxford: Oxford University Press.

Harman, G. (1965). "Inference to the best explanation," *Philosophical Review* **74**.

Harman, G. (1977). *The Nature of Morality*, New York: Oxford University Press.

220   *Bibliography*

Harman, G. (1980). "Relativistic ethics: morality as politics," *Midwest Studies in Philosophy* **3**: 109–28.

Harman, G. (1983). "Justice and moral bargaining," *Social Philosophy and Policy* **1**.

Harman, G. (1986). *Change in View: Principles of Reasoning* Cambridge, Massachusetts: Bradford Books/MIT Press.

Harman, G. (1987). "(Nonsolipsistic) conceptual role semantics." In Ernest LePore (ed.), *New Directions in Semantics* (London: Academic Press), pp. 55–81.

Harman, G. (1990). "Immanent and transcendent approaches to the theory of meaning." In Roger Gibson and Robert B. Barrett (eds), *Perspectives on Quine* (Oxford: Blackwell), pp. 144–57.

Harman, G. (1991). "Moral diversity as an argument for moral relativism," in Douglas Odegard and Carole Stewart, *Perspectives on Moral Relativism* (Milliken, Ontario: Agathon) pp. 13–31.

Harman, G. (1993a). "Meaning holism defended," *Grazer Philosophische Studien* **46**: 163–71.

Harman, G. (1993b). "Can science understand the mind?" in *Conceptions of the Mind: Essays in Honor of George A. Miller*, edited by Gilbert Harman, (Hillside, New Jersey: Lawrence Erlbaum), pp. 111–21.

Harman, G. (1994). "Explaining values," *Social Philosophy and Policy* **11**: 229–48. Reprinted in Ellen Frankel Paul, Fred D. Miller, Jr., and Jeffrey Paul (eds), *Cultural Pluralism and Moral Knowledge* (Cambridge: Cambridge University Press, 1994).

Horwich, P. (1990). *Truth*, London: Blackwell.

Horwich, P. (1993). "Gibbard's theory of norms," *Philosophy and Public Affairs* **22**: 67–78.

Hume, D. (1739). *Treatise on Human Nature*, Book III, Part 2, Section 2.

Hume, D. (1757). "Of the Standard of Taste," *Essays: Moral, Political, and Literary*, ed. T. H. Green and T. H. Grose, Darmstadt, Germany: Scientia Verlag Aalen, 1964.

Johnston, M., (1989). "Dispositional theories of value," *Proceedings of the Aristotelian Society*, Supplementary **63**: 139–74.

Kim, J. (1993). *Supervenience and Mind*, Cambridge: Cambridge University Press.

Kittay, E. F. and Meyers, D. T. (eds), (1987). *Women and Moral Theory*, Totowa, New Jersey: Rowman and Littlefield.

Kohlberg, L. (1981). *Essays on Moral Development*, volume 1, The *Philosophy of Moral Development: Moral Stages and the Idea of Justice*, San Francisco: Harper and Row.

Lewis, D. (1989). "Dispositional theories of value," *Proceedings of the Aristotelian Society*, Supplementary **63**: 113–37.

Lyons, D. (1976). "Ethical relativism and the problem of incoherence," *Ethics* **86**: 107–21, reprinted in *Relativism*, ed. Jack W. Meiland and Michael Krausz, Notre Dame: University of Notre Dame Press, 1982.

Mackie, J. (1977). *Ethics: Inventing Right and Wrong*, London: Penguin Books.

Miller, R. W. (1992). *Moral Differences: Truth, Justice and Conscience in a World of Conflict*, Princeton, New Jersey: Princeton University Press.

Moore, G. E. (1903): G. E. Moore, *Principia Ethica*, Thomas Baldwin (ed.), Cambridge: Cambridge University Press, 1993.

Mothersill, M. (1984). *Beauty Restored*, Oxford: Clarendon Press.

Mothersill, M. (1989). "Hume and the paradox of taste," *Aesthetics: A Critical Anthology*, ed. George Dickie, Richard Sclafani, and Ronald Roblin, New York: St. Martin's Press.

Nagel, T. (1970). *The Possibility of Altruism*, Oxford: Oxford University Press.

Nozick, R. (1972). *Anarchy, State, and Utopia*, New York: Basic Books.

Oakes, J. (1983). *The Ruling Race*, New York: Vintage Books.

Piaget, J. (1956). *The Moral Judgment of the Child*, New York: The Free Press.

Platts, M. (1980). "Moral realism and the end of desire," in Mark Platts (ed.), *Reference, Truth, and Reality*, Boston: Routledge & Kegan Paul.

Price, H. (1988). *Facts and the Function of Truth*, Oxford: Basil Blackwell.

Prior, Arthur N. (1976). "The autonomy of ethics." In Prior A. N., *Papers in Logic and Ethics* (London: Duckworth) pp. 88–96.

Quinn, W. (1986). "Truth and explanation in ethics," *Ethics* **96**, reprinted in Warren Quinn, *Morality and Action*, Cambridge: Cambridge University Press, 1993.

Rachels, J. (1975). "Active and passive euthanasia," *New England Journal of Medicine* **292**.

Railton, P. (1986). "Moral realism," *Philosophical Review* **95**.

Rawls, J. (1971). *A Theory of Justice*, Cambridge, Mass.: Harvard University Press.

Ringer, R. J. (1977). *Looking Out for Number One*, New York: Fawcett Crest Books.

Shafer-Landau, R. (1994). "Ethical disagreement, ethical objectivism and moral indeterminacy," *Philosophy and Phenomenological Research* **54**.

Silberbauer, G. (1993). "Ethics in small-scale societies," *A Companion to Ethics*, ed. Peter Singer, Oxford: Blackwell.

Singer, P. (1972). "Famine, affluence, and morality," *Philosophy and Public Affairs* 1.

Singer, P. (1975). *Animal Liberation*, New York: Random House.

Stevenson, C. L. (1937). "The emotive meaning of ethical terms," *Mind* 46, reprinted in Stevenson (1963).

Stevenson, C. L. (1945). *Ethics and Language* (New Haven, Conn.: Yale University Press.)

Stevenson, C. L., (1963). *Facts and Values*, New Haven and London, Yale University Press.

Stevenson, C. L. (1963a). "The nature of ethical disagreement," in Stevenson (1963), pp. 1–9.

Stevenson, C. L. (1963b). "Relativism and nonrelativism in the theory of value," in Stevenson (1963).

Stoljar, D. (1993). "Emotivism and truth conditions," *Philosophical Studies* 70: 81–101.

Sturgeon, N. (1985). "Moral explanations," in David Copp and David Zimmerman (eds), *Morality, Reason and Truth* (Totowa, N.J.: Rowan and Allanheld, reprinted in Geoffrey Sayre-McCord's anthology, *Essays on Moral Realism*, Ithaca: Cornell Press, 1988.

Sturgeon, N. (1986). "Harman on moral explanations of natural facts," *Spindel Conference: Moral Realism, Southern Journal of Philosophy* 24, Supplement.

Thomson, J. (1986). *Rights Restitution, and Risk: Essays, in Moral Theory*, edited by William Parent, Cambridge, Mass.: Harvard University Press, 1986, chapter 6, "Killing, letting die, and the trolley problem," and chapter 7, "The trolley problem."

Thomson, J. (1990). *The Realm of Rights*, Cambridge, Mass.: Harvard University Press.

Thomson, J. (1992). "On some ways in which a thing can be good.," *Social Philosophy & Policy* 9: 96–117.

Thomson, J. (1994). "Goodness and utilitarianism," *Proceedings and Addresses of The American Philosophical Association* 67.4: 7–21.

Trivers, R. L. (1971). "The evolution of reciprocal altruism," *Quarterly Review of Biology* 46: 35–57.

von Wright, G. H. (1963). *The Varieties of Goodness* (London: Routledge & Kegan Paul.

Walzer, M. (1987). *Interpretation and Social Criticism*, Cambridge, Massachusetts: Harvard University Press.

Wiggins, D. (1976). "Truth, invention, and the meaning of life," *Proceedings of the British Academy* LXII (1976), reprinted in David

Wiggins, *Needs, Values, Truth*, second edition, Oxford UK & Cambridge Mass.: Blackwell, 1991.

Wong, D. B. (1984). *Moral Relativity*, Berkeley, California: University of California Press.

Ziff, P. (1960). *Semantic Analysis*, Ithaca: Cornell University Press.

Index